I believe in you, _____.
You CAN face each challenge and be triumphant
in Turning Setbacks into Comebacks!

# Fully Armed

## Ron Gustafson
### with Bob Schaller

Fully Armed

Ron Gustafson with Bob Schaller, Fully Armed

ISBN 1-887002-97-9

Cross Training Publishing
317 West Second Street
Grand Island, NE 68801
(308) 384-5762

This book is manufactured in the United States of America.

Library of Congress Cataloging in Publication Data in Progress.

Published by Cross Training Publishing,
317 West Second Street
Grand Island, NE 68801

# DEDICATION

With love I dedicate this book to my wife, Julie, and our three children, Isaac, Josiah and Hannah. You are all constantly encouraging and challenging me to be all that God wants me to be. Thank you for believing in me and making "Fully Armed" possible. I love you!

# CONTENTS

# Foreword

When I think of Ron "Gus" Gustafson, the words courage and determination come to mind.

I also think of the word "faith" because of Gus's trust in God, particularly during Gus's ordeal as a young man - who as a 9-year-old had his arm ripped off by a piece of farm equipment. Horrendous as it was, his perspective is heart-warming.

Gus is not about simply persevering - indeed, it goes much deeper than that. Gus is all about overcoming obstacles, and that in itself is the essence of who he is.

Upon meeting Gus, another word that comes to mind is tenacity. That is the amazing message Gus gives to other people. His faith has given him the spirit to move forward.

I lost my arm to cancer when I was pitching for the San Francisco Giants. I was blessed to have an arm for as long as I did, and when I lost my arm, I knew it was for a reason - to touch other people's lives and use my faith and story to help people find it within themselves to rise to the challenges they face.

Gus is also using his story to make an impact on people. He is always upbeat: His common phrase of "make it a great day," or how he says "fantastic!" when you ask him how he's doing shows the attitude that has helped him help so many people. Regardless of the size, shape or placing of the obstacle, he continues to press on. That is what encouragement is all about, and Gus exudes encouragement when he travels and tells his story. And his story is so needed in our society today.

We put a story about Gus in my book, "Portraits of Courage." When I went through the different articles, I was amazed at his willingness to move on and to excel at whatever he did. He went after life in a way many people in his situation would not because they might be too devastated to see the light. I think this speaks volumes about Gus's faith, and the fact that Gus has an understanding about what God intended for his life.

Once you get to know Gus, you see how important it is to have the family and friends he had around him, and continues to have. What he went through would debilitate people who do not have the family, friends, teachers, coaches and spiritual folks to help carry them on. That is where I am convinced God has shown Gus faithfulness - through the blessing of those around him.

It is really important to understand what drives and motivates a man to be what he is. Underneath all the things Gus has done is a faith in God that has motivated Gus to do what he has done as a boy, a man, a husband, a brother, a son and an encourager to others.

The phrase "never give up" is one that is taken too lightly because it is often thrown around without direction or explanation. In essence, Gus's life and story will motivate people, like never before, to never give up. The reality Gus exemplifies is that if you do not give up, God will not give up on you.

Gus's story and example will motivate and encourage anyone facing a serious challenge to see it through!

**Dave Dravecky**
*Former San Francisco Giants pitcher*

# ACKNOWLEDGMENTS

Julie, my wife, has been a trooper through all the emotions of writing this book. My life seems to be an emotional roller coaster, and Julie is a pillar of stability and strength. She is wise, strong, and loving. Thank you for putting up with me on this long journey. I am Fully Armed because she is part of my life.

I am so grateful to the greatest mom and dad in the world, Don and Joyce Gustafson. They modeled a life of love, integrity and selflessness in front of me each day while I was growing up. Now that Julie and I have children, I can better understand the true pain and concern that they lived with during and following my accident. Thank you for setting the bar so high for me as a parent.

A huge thank you to my brothers, Rick, Mike and Jim, who were always there to push me, encourage me and also taught me to compete in all aspects of life. Their standard of excellence demonstrated in athletics and life set the mark that I shoot for on a daily basis. When tragedy struck our family, they could have chosen to be jealous or spiteful and turned away from me, but they chose to draw closer to me and make our family stronger. You guys are the greatest!

Bob Schaller has been a treat to work with in writing Fully Armed. He has had to deal with my late night phone calls and my constant demands in completing this book. Bob has been there with words of encouragement when I needed to be reminded to think BIG!

Above all, I am grateful to my Lord and Savior, Jesus Christ, for loving me and dying for me. He is my endless source of hope strength and joy. May He be glorified and honored with Fully Armed.

# 1

---

# The Dreamer

We live in the greatest age of opportunity. We have opportunities and challenges that many people never get to experience. We all have the ability to dream, but very few take the time to dream. Our dreams are what make each of us unique and give us the direction and emotion for our lives.

I'm a dreamer. I always have been a dreamer, and always will be. I grew up on a small family farm near Lyons, Nebraska, and had numerous opportunities to grow and learn in a great environment. We raised mostly corn and a little bit of wheat and beans on the rolling hills of northeast Nebraska.

My father's real love for farming and ranching was his cattle. He used to pull his old 1977 Chevy pickup with rust and dents to the top of one of the hills overlooking a pasture and turn off the motor. He sat with us and simply said, "Isn't that beautiful?" We looked down into the valley where the stream ran out of our neighbor's pasture into ours and formed a creek. It ran down the valley and eventually into a dam. The pasture was deep green and baby calves kicked up their heels and ran and played. They chased each other for hours. The mothers would lie in the deep grass chewing their cud in a totally relaxed state. As the sun got hotter during the day, the cows eventually found themselves submerged in the cool water of the dam. Dad could watch their activities for hours.

I was always relieved when he attempted to start the old Chevy and it actually started again. It amazed me that he could get that old thing up to 50 miles per hour with all that silicone glue and Nebraska chrome on it (duct tape).

My brothers and I were always going down to the tree-lined creek to play war, cops and robbers or just to go exploring. We climbed trees, dug forts, watched animals and their babies, and found some of the neatest treasurers imaginable. I think it was once said that one person's garbage might be someone else's treasure. There was such freedom in the simplicity of running, jumping, and exploring in what seemed to be a massive territory, called our farm.

There were a few times when my brothers "helped" me into the creek and I walked home sopping wet with mud up to my waist. At times, I thought being the youngest and smallest member of an all-boy family was punishment for some unknown sin. Mom learned to expect a rough type of behavior from her four boys. Visits to the local doctor's office seemed to be the norm.

Our home was a ranch-style built on top of a hill. Trees surrounded the house for a windbreak. We had a huge, beautiful barn where the cattle in the feed lot took shelter during the tough Nebraska winters. Part of the barn was used for storing bales of hay and straw in the loft. I used to crawl up there, swing out over the loose hay and bales from a rope that was tied to the top rafters, let go and land in a soft pile of straw. When Mom came out to the barn looking for us, we hid in the straw and jumped out and yelled at the top of our lungs to scare her. I can still see her inhale and put her hand over her chest as we startled her. There were so many great memories on the farm.

As a young boy, I would lay on top of a haystack, gaze into the sky and dream about becoming an All-American

running back for the Nebraska Cornhuskers. I would dream
of the emotion of the game-winning play: The Huskers—as
they are referred to with affection by native Nebraskans—
huddled up on the 15-yard line. The radio announcer's voice
was clear in my head:

"The crazy Cornhusker crowd is roaring with the
expectation of a game-winning touchdown. The call is for the
All-American I-back to receive the pitch from the
quarterback and run off tackle. There are 10 seconds left in
the game, the Huskers down by 5 points with the ball on the
11-yard line. Just as the play was designed, Ron Gustafson
receives the pitch, waits for the pulling guard to push the
defensive end to the outside and 'Gus' cuts back to the
middle, spins off the linebacker, and runs right over the
cornerback and dives into the end zone for the game-winning
touchdown with no time remaining on the clock!"

The crowd roared, my family glowed with pride and NFL
scouts jotted their notes on their clipboards, eager to know
who would get this Gustafson kid in the NFL draft.

It appeared that I had been equipped with all the tools
needed to turn that dream of playing professional football
into a reality. My family was very athletic. I was very gifted as
an 8-year-old third-grader competing in baseball and
basketball with kids three and four years older. I had great
speed, was the biggest kid in my class and simply loved
athletics and the challenge it brought. I was fortunate to be
the youngest of four boys in a very athletic family. My big
brothers, Rick and Mike, were 10 and nine years older than
me, and Jim was five years my senior.

Athletics were a built-in activity at the Gustafson
household. It seemed to be a basic need along with food,
water, and sleep. The sun never went down without a
competitive game of baseball, basketball or football. The key

word in the Gustafson family was "competition." All of us thrived on the competitive nature in each of us. Meals were won by eating the most in the least amount of time. Chores were won by being the first one up in the morning and by carrying the heaviest bucket or bushel basket of corn as we fed our livestock.

Our front yard became the greatest football stadium in the country. My brothers played defense. I wedged the football under my right arm and tried to run between them as fast as I could. Rick's target was my right knee, Mike's target was my left rib cage and Jim hit me anywhere he pleased.

My body would be airborne and end up face down in the grass with three big brothers lovingly rubbing my face in the dirt. They always made sure I had plenty of dirt and grass in my face when I was down. They kept telling me that this would make me tough and a better player.

There were times when I was so angry I had to prove to them that I was going to be a great running back, and that I could run through them and anyone else who got in the way. The next attempt had the same result; me face down with a mouth full of dirt and grass. Occasionally I got hurt. Tears welled up in my eyes and my brothers made fun of me and said that great running backs never cried. Being young and naïve, I believed them. I bit my lip, held back the tears and funneled the pain and frustration into the next attempt. Just when I was at the point of being discouraged, hurt, and totally exhausted, my brothers would hit me. I bounced off the first would-be tackler, spun to avoid the linebacker's hit and scored the big touchdown. The three of them were in a heap and I danced in the end zone celebrating with a fist in the air. At that moment, it was as if I could hear the crowd and the rush of energy one gets when the unobtainable goal is reached. This also created the energy to try to run through them a hundred more times.

My brothers always knew when their little brother needed to win, even though the winning opportunities were few and far between. They were master motivators for their little brother. They knew what got me charged me up and what buttons to push to make me tap into my peak performance.

Some of our neighbors and friends thought my brothers were mean and overly competitive with me. They were extremely rough and forced me to play up to their level. This was one of the greatest things they ever did for me and it paid huge dividends in the years ahead. The fundamental philosophy of "going to the next level" has been invaluable in my pursuit of excellence.

The importance and application of dreams, emotions and teachable moments are what I hope to relay in this book. So many of the stories that I will share are very personal and bring tears to my eyes. I enjoy the emotion of each moment. It allows me to relive the moments, good or bad, and remember the feelings, the adrenaline, the pain, the tears, but most of all, the triumph of those moments.

On Oct. 6, 1996, the Nebraska High School Sports Hall of Fame presented to me the "Ron Gustafson Inspiration Award." The award is given to the outstanding high school athlete in Nebraska who has overcome huge obstacles, yet has achieved great success on the athletic field. I was very honored and humbled by being the first recipient—and the namesake—of this award.

I stood on the stage in the Lincoln (NE) Station Banquet Hall surrounded by great high school athletes who were being inducted into the Nebraska Sports Hall of Fame. I reflected back to the days in the haystack where I dreamed of fame, fortune and a career as an all-star running back in the National Football League. The dream never materialized, but here I was being honored for great athletic abilities after overcoming great challenges.

As I was introduced, the crowd stood and began to applaud, a standing ovation for that small-town farm kid, the dreamer. Many of the other inductees that night had lived out their dream to reality. They became collegiate athletes and very good professional athletes. What was it about Ron Gustafson and what he had overcome that made a crowd rise to its feet and applaud?

### The honor I received was a beautiful plaque that read:

*Ron Gustafson*
*Who as an athlete at Lyons High School*
*1980-1984*
*Achieved outstanding athletic success*
*By overcoming monumental obstacles.*
*Your never-give-up attitude*
*And your accomplishments have been an*
*Inspiration to those around you.*
*This award will be presented annually in*
*Your name to recognize others in high school athletics.*
*October 6, 1996*

The plaque was presented to me, the pictures were taken and the microphone was handed to me to say a few words. I looked out over the crowd and saw my dad. My father is a 6-foot-6-inch, 265-pound teddy bear. He has very dark rough skin from all the tough days working on the farm. He's a very intimidating figure for most people, but a warm, gentle and kind man to those who are close to him. I am so fortunate to have such a great man as my father, teacher and example. My eyes are naturally drawn to his even in a crowd of hundreds of people.

Dad is a man of few words, but when he speaks, those around him listen and apply what he says. I have such trust and respect for him. He is one of very few people I know who loves what he does for a living and would be doing the same job whether he was paid $10,000 a year or $1,000,000 a year. He taught me so many lessons growing up and I continue to apply his wisdom to my life today.

Then I saw a beautiful, warm, caring woman seated next to my father. My mother is truly the wind under Dad's wings—the mother of four, an educator in the school system for 30 years and the glue that kept our family together. She is the woman who will drop whatever she is doing to help the kids, neighbors or friends. Her heart is always warm and willing to serve. Mom carried quite a load in our home full of boys. While the rest of the family was blessed athletically, Mom, well, she was blessed musically.

My brothers were seated around the same table with my parents. As I addressed the crowd, the same brothers who were rubbing my face in the dirt 21 years ago were now glowing with pride as their little brother received the honor that would carry his name for years to come.

Rick, the oldest, was a great baseball player. He was a two-sport athlete at Midland College in Fremont, Nebraska, playing both basketball and baseball. He was small physically as a high school student, but always had the determination to compete. He developed his muscular, granite-like physique after college as he took up power lifting.

Mike went from a 6-foot, 185-pound defensive back his freshman year at Augustana College in Sioux Falls, S.D., to a 6-foot, 3-inch, 250-pound tight end. He set school records in the weight room and on the football field. Mike worked harder than anyone I've ever known. He has always been hungry for success on and off the athletic field.

Jim was a stand-out point guard on the basketball team in high school and one of the greatest passers and ball handlers I've ever seen play. He spent most of his college career at the University of North Dakota and finished his career at Hastings (NE) College. He was blessed with leaping ability and endurance to run all day.

That night at the hall of fame banquet, as they were glowing with pride, I was welling up with tears, trying to express the thanks to my parents for giving up so much for my sake and always being there when I needed them. The rush of emotion was overwhelming. My family had sacrificed so much for me while I was growing up.

Many kids grow up today wanting to be Michael Jordan, Shaquille O'Neal or Kobe Bryant. I grew up in a house filled with great athletes. My dream was to some day be as good as my brothers. My daily challenges consisted of trying to compete successfully against my idols—my brothers.

# 2

## When the Dreams Seem to Disappear

My hometown of Lyons is a small town of 1,000 people. Our main street was truly "Main Street" because all the businesses were on a stretch of three blocks. At one time, Lyons was truly a thriving "mini-metropolis" in northeast Nebraska.

In many cases, everyone else knew what you were doing before you knew what you were doing. This is the small-town mystique that is still alive and well today.

My dad was well known for driving the oldest, most beat up pick-up in the area. He also was known for having his small boys following right behind him, similar to the ducklings following the mother duck. Everywhere he went, he had a trail of boys stumbling and pestering each other right behind him.

I got to tag along with my dad to the feed store, the hardware store, the Allis Chalmers implement dealership and then to the coffee shop. The coffee shop was an interesting place for a young boy. I heard about all the action of the day in a farmer's life. If it were raining outside, the grumpy old farmers complained because it was too wet. If it were hot and dry outside, they talked about how miserable the weather was for the crops. I loved the coffee shop and hearing the old farmers talk about the farm and ranch markets, share tips for success and spin yarns and tell anecdotes.

The routine has transitioned to the sons who took over the farm for their dads. Now those same farmers who I listened to can be found at the coffee shop comparing snapshots of their grandchildren.

As I grew up, I began to see the personalities of the farmers come out by the way they wore their hats and by the wear and tear on the pliers holster attached to the belts on their hips.

I also learned that there was no pleasing a farmer. That is, the work ethic and quest to either make ends meet, or turn an average crop into a bumper crop, was driven by an insatiable appetite to live by the Midwest work ethic. They worked hard and long. Nothing ever turned out exactly how they wanted it. Yet they pushed forward, through hailstorms and broken down equipment, striving to feed the American people while hoping to make enough money to cover the note for their property at the bank—and maybe have enough left over to repair the farm equipment which is passed down through generations like city folk hand down clothes.

All one could do is laugh at the stories and smile at the atmosphere created around the big table at the coffee shop.

Mom was teaching during the days and I worked with Dad before I was old enough to go to school. I rode with him in the tractors and combine and worked right along side of him, usually slowing him down in each task and often frustrating him with my curiosity. The afternoons would roll around and I took my naps on the floor of the tractor as Dad worked the fields. It was dusty, dirty, and rough and were some of my favorite memories. I loved to be with Dad. I had the opportunity to see him succeed and struggle through the day and how he responded to the challenges and circumstances around him. What a great lab for learning!

Our school in Lyons was a fine old building. The high

school, junior high and elementary schools were all in the same physical building. The staircases creaked as you walked down the steps and the floors moaned as you walked across them.

The school was a three-story brick building. The original structure sported a new addition, the biggest portion being a big, beautiful gymnasium. I loved the smell of the gym when I first walked in. It had the pull-out bleachers and the baskets that folded up out of the line of sight so the stage on the east end could be used for musicals and plays.

I really enjoyed the small town school. As an elementary student, I had the opportunity to interact with high school students to see what they were doing and how they were acting. In a small town, the eyes that are watching are sometimes a deterrent to poor behavior. The small school environment was a great asset for me. I was able to see my brothers during the day and truly know my teachers and the faculty at school.

My fourth-grade teacher, Jerry Mathers, was the best. He made learning so much fun. I was always challenged by him and encouraged to always do my best.

One day Mr. Mathers was finishing our history class when the lunch bell rang. I tore out of the room and flew down two flights of stairs while taking three steps at a time. My speed and agility had served me well once again and it had taken me to the first-place position in line for lunch, one of the most prized positions in life. All my buddies and I jockeyed for that first-place spot. We were always competitive and wanted to be first at everything we did, even the lunch line.

We had great cooks at school who always served up the meal with a smile.

My brothers had a great reputation in our community and

school, so I had to live up to the Gustafson tradition. My smiles and thank yous to the cooks along with a wink every now and then always generated the biggest piece of pizza and apple crisp. I was a growing boy and needed all the food I could get during the day. Janice Lane was the head cook and spoiled me rotten.

We all ate as fast as we could so we could make it out to the playground where some very serious football was played. Mr. Mathers refereed our games and taught us the fundamentals as we played.

Mr. Mathers was a great teacher, motivator and sports enthusiast, but some of his calls on the playground were horrendous! I still get after him about some of those historic calls. He divided the teams so that the speed and size were equal. I couldn't wait to receive the opening kick off. After competing against my brothers, playing against kids my own age was a piece of cake. The goal was to score each time I touched the ball.

I received the kick-off and took off running, sometimes running by tacklers, other times running right through them. Scoring was automatic. My size, speed, strength and athletic abilities seemed to be years ahead of my classmates.

Our lunch hour ended and my team would win by a large margin. We were herded back into school as we jostled for bragging rights of the noon football playoffs. Mr. Mathers had quite a chore getting us plugged back into a classroom setting.

Afternoon classes were always tough for me. I was a clock-watcher who waited and listened with anticipation for the last bell of the day to ring to release us from school.

On Sept. 9, 1975, at 3:15 p.m. the bell finally rang and it was the sweetest ring of the day. This meant a bus ride home, working with Dad on the farm, playing some ball and having steaks for supper. What else could a 9-year-old farm boy want from life?

I opened the door leading out of the classroom. I once again bolted down the steps, taking three or four steps at a time and ran out of the school building. It was a gorgeous day. The sun was bright, the sky was crystal blue and there was a cool breeze. I jumped on the bus where the driver, Mr. Middendorf, greeted me with a smile as he did every day and asked how my day was. I always said, "Fantastic." The bus began to roll away from school and we started the route.

Our farm is three miles from Lyons—two miles east and one mile north. The bus traveled east two miles and I hopped off of the bus and ran the last mile to our farm. This was all part of the daily regimen. In my mind, this mile run would make me faster, stronger and allow me to become a better athlete. I loved to do things the hard way, always striving to become a great athlete. It seemed like I always took the difficult path so I could become both mentally and physically tough.

I ran into the house, sweaty and thirsty, took the stairs to my basement bedroom and followed orders. "Change out of your school clothes and put on your work clothes." After I changed, I ran back upstairs, grabbed a couple cookies ("Scooby snacks") that Mom baked the weekend before, chugged a big glass of milk and headed to see where my father was.

As I ran out of the house I could hear the sound of the Oliver 88 tractor starting up in the barn. Dad was pulling the tractor out and filling the feeder wagon with silage to feed the cattle. Dad went through the same procedures he had done every day since he could remember. He pulled the feeder wagon over to the grain bin, put just the right amount of corn into the wagon, got on the loader tractor, drove over to the hay stacks, grabbed a load of hay and dumped it into the feeder wagon. He then parked the loader tractor, got on the

Oliver 88 and drove the tractor and feeder wagon up in front of the house. He crept to a stop and then signaled for me to jump on just as we had done thousands of times before.

The Oliver 88 was an old reliable tractor my dad had had for years. Its only purpose on the farm was to pull the feeder wagon each day to feed the cattle. Its engine started on the coldest of Nebraska winter mornings and was "old reliable." We loved that old tractor. It seemed to have its own personality.

Dad was in the driver's seat and I jumped up onto the tractor and sat facing his right side on the moon-shaped fender that was over the right rear tire. We pulled onto the road, carefully looking for traffic. Dad pulled the throttle open and we were sailing down the road.

Dad began the conversation and asked how my day had been. It was always important for me to tell him about the noon recess and some of the plays we ran for big yardage on the football field.

What could be better than this? A beautiful day, working outside with Dad and telling him about my day, looking at the sun shining, the rolling hills filled with corn and beans, and cattle and horses grazing on the pasture land along the road.

We went down the first hill and began to climb the second hill. Suddenly I felt my body being thrown to the ground. Everything was in slow motion as I felt the impact of the ground, gravel and dirt flying onto my face and the sound of the tractor's engine coming to a halt. It felt as though I were a rag doll being violently thrown to the ground. As I relive the moment, it seemed to be a nightmare as the wheel flew off the tractor and I fell directly under the rear axle. I remember falling to the ground, bouncing up a bit and the impact of something heavy and out of control rushing over my body.

Dad fought to stay in control of the tractor but could not handle the out-of-control machine. He can still picture me falling off the tractor and its hub about to run across my throat. By God's grace, my body suddenly flipped and turned when the hub ran across my shoulder while my head snapped out of the way of the iron hub at the last second.

Everything came to a crashing halt. All of a sudden, the feeling of being on top of the world and being in control took a 180-degree turn. My body was in pieces, in a ditch, covered with silage, grass, dirt and gravel, and I was, though alive, bleeding profusely.

The hub on the rim of the wheel of the "old reliable" had broken and the wheel had fallen off. It happened to be the right rear wheel right below where I was riding on the fender.

Dad held on as long as he could but was eventually launched away from the tractor and landed in the ditch approximately 15 yards away. I can recall the pain in his voice as he ran back to me yelling my name, "Ronnie! Ronnie! Ronnie!"

Dad picked me up out of the ditch. My right arm and shoulder had been torn off my body and my lower right leg was mangled. Under such distress, my father still had the presence of mind to grab my right ankle as he picked me up. The only thing that kept my right foot attached to the rest of my body was a strip of skin an inch wide in the back of my leg and some mangled muscles and ligaments just below my knee.

My father pressed my right shoulder—where the arm had been torn off—against his chest as he ran home, carrying his bloody and mangled little boy. My life was truly in his hands. As he held me next to his chest, it seemed as though his heart was pumping life through me, sustaining me.

I recall looking up at Dad; the firm, tough old farmer, and seeing for the first time in my life, fear in his eyes.

He was beaten up from the fall he had endured and was terrified to see his son literally torn up by an out-of-control farm vehicle. Imagine what went through his mind at this time.

I remained conscious through the whole scene. I talked to Dad as he ran the quarter of a mile back to our house on that long, lonely gravel road. I wasn't aware at the time of the magnitude of the damage to my body.

I was crying. Dad was crying. I looked at him and said "Dad, if I die...I want you to know that I love you. Please make sure Mom and my brothers know that I love them, too."

Dad kept reassuring me that I was going to live...that I could make it. He held on to me with such strength and love. My body was truly a rag doll. I had no energy or ability to move. The whole scene seemed to be a terrible dream and I would wake up anytime.

Mom was on the phone with my brother Rick, who was a sophomore at Midland College, when she heard my father's desperate yells. She hung up the phone and rushed to see what was wrong. Dad threw open the door and yelled for her to call the rescue squad. He kept saying, "I've killed Ronnie! I've killed Ronnie!" Mom began to ask a question when Dad responded "Call the rescue squad!" and turned back to me.

Dad laid me down in the front yard.

Mom called the rescue number, and it seemed to ring an eternity without an answer. She hung up and tried again, but there was still no answer. She called the operator who finally got through to the rescue unit.

After my mother was put through to them, my father carried me in the door and laid me down on the living room floor. I was literally bleeding to death before my parents' very eyes as I crept closer to death. I knew as well as my parents did that my chances of surviving were slim and growing slimmer with each moment. I felt as though I were saying my last good-bye to my Mom and Dad, who loved me so much.

To attempt to slow the bleeding, Mom covered my leg and also put some towels that she had grabbed from the kitchen cabinet in the gaping hole on my shoulder, where my right arm had been torn away from my body.

I was conscious and had the presence of mind to tell Mom not to cry. I assured her, in a very calm voice, that I would be fine. Mom was praying and pleading with God.

Within minutes, the rescue squad arrived and loaded me up. Mom rode in the front of the rescue squad as Jon Heideman drove the ambulance and Dad was in the back with me. We headed down the road. There was a small hospital in Oakland, just 10 miles away, but they knew the Oakland hospital was unable to handle an accident like this, so we headed for Omaha, which is another 60 miles south.

Just south of Oakland, a car pulled out in front of us. We had our lights on but not the sirens. If we were to put the sirens on, we would probably have scared the driver and that would have slowed us down even more. We finally got around the car and continued.

Lee Appleby, one of the emergency medical technicians, put a blood pressure cuff on my arm. He pumped up the cuff and it showed my blood pressure was normal. They thought there was something wrong with the cuff because I had lost a lot of blood and my blood pressure could not have been normal. They tried another cuff and my blood pressure was truly normal. This was one of many unexplained miracles in my life.

As we proceeded, Jon, the driver, realized I would not live

to see Omaha. He decided to take me to the Dodge County Memorial Hospital in Fremont, instead. He radioed ahead and made them aware of my condition.

Mom turned around and talked to us in the back of the ambulance. Dad had a fearful look on his face while I was very calm and tearless. I continued to talk to Lee Appleby and my dad while we traveled. I don't know why, but in such a bizarre setting, all I could think to talk about was sports, and I assured everyone in the ambulance that I was going to be a great athlete, whatever the circumstances.

We pulled into the hospital in Fremont. They unloaded me and wheeled me into the emergency room. I remember leaving my mother and father in the waiting room. As I was rolled away, they knew that they may never see me again—at least not alive.

I entered the emergency room and the medical staff began to cut off my clothing and to clean off some of the dirt, gravel, debris and blood.

**Following are the thoughts and recollections of rescue volunteer, Lee Appleby:**

"As in most rural Nebraska small towns in 1975, volunteers filled the ranks of the local fire department and rescue squad. When an emergency occurred in that era, a summons for help was usually telephoned to the county sheriff's 24-hour dispatcher, who in turn, notified the emergency units in the nearest community. In Lyons that September afternoon, the town siren wailed a lengthy alert about 5 p.m. and three men—myself, Jon Heideman and Dick Strehle, available Lyons Volunteer Fire Department members—responded as quickly as circumstances permitted. The first step after arriving at the fire hall was to contact the county dispatcher for directions and information about the initial call.

"We learned there had been a tractor accident at the Don

Gustafson farm. One of Don's boys was injured. With that scant information, we piled into the squad and headed east of town. In a small community like Lyons, answering an emergency call often involved people you knew. Each of the squad members knew Don and Joyce and each of their four sons, Rick, Mike, Jim and 9-year-old Ronnie. I remember my feelings on the way to the Gustafson farm well. The three-mile trip seemed to take a long time. We didn't know what we were going to find when we arrived. As we pulled off the gravel road and approached the driveway of the ranch-style home, there was no one outside. I exited the Suburban van while grabbing the trauma bag and ran toward the three cement steps flanked by wrought iron railings. The front door opened and Don appeared. The look on his face was one that only a parent whose child is seriously injured can have. Don is an imposing man by any standard. His Scandinavian heritage is reflected in his 265-pound, 6-foot, 6-inch frame. Before my foot hit the first step Don seemed to tower before me, his shirt covered with blood from carrying an injured Ron to the house, pointing his callused finger at me commanding, 'You've got to stop the bleeding.'

"I entered the living room. Ron was lying on the floor, covered with blankets. His mother, Joyce, hovered nearby. Lyons physician Dr. C.M. Hadley had been summoned from his nearby country home and was already on the scene. When I pulled the blanket back to assess the injury, I saw the shoulder and arm had been severed from Ronnie's torso. I was amazed, considering the severity of his wounds, that he was conscious and aware of things going on around him. By this time the bleeding had almost stopped. The flow had decreased because of low blood pressure, and because the severed arm had been pinched rather than cut off by the thick iron wheel rim of the tractor. His leg injury, at that point, was of secondary concern. We applied dressings to the wounds. It was decided that Ron was to be transported to the Dodge County Memorial Hospital in Fremont, 40 miles away. We allowed Ron's parents to accompany their young son in the small squad for two reasons: They were not about to be separated from Ron and I was not sure he would make it to the hospital alive. Ron stayed conscious during the half-hour trip to the hospital. Because of the limited space in the van's cot area, his dad and I rode in the rear with Ron. I will never forget the many times during that ride he said, "Dad, I'm still going to play ball."

Ron was talking about playing ball. I was wondering if he would live. We arrived at the hospital emergency room. The squad personnel relayed pertinent information to doctors and Ron was whisked into surgery. In most cases, the squad members return home at this point. This instance, however, was more traumatic than most.

"Word had not yet reached other family members. Don and Joyce were alone and I was reluctant to leave them. I opted to stay with them and the squad went back to Lyons. Those who have lived through the dreadful hours of waiting out a critical surgery know the range of emotions a parent suffers. Don voiced feelings of guilt and frustration. He was heartsick; taking needless blame and mistakenly assuming the farm accident was his fault. That tragic night the father of four sports-loving sons worried Ron would not be able to participate in athletics. Only a few years later Ron would prove otherwise. The day of that accident I learned from a 9-year-old boy about determination, courage and the will to live. In the years that followed the accident, Ron's accomplishments in sports and his personal life have made true his words, 'Dad, I'm still going to play ball!'"

# 3

## The Will to Live

It was early evening as the emergency room staff began the task of saving my life. The lights were bright, I was still conscious and taking in all that was being said and done. My body was in a state of shock but my mind was still processing the information around me.

Mom and Dad were in the emergency waiting room. Lee Appleby stayed with them. Dad was frantic and continued to blame himself for what had happened, as would anyone in similar circumstances. Dad had always been such a strong self-sustaining man. Now, his world had caved in around him and all control and understanding had been lost.

Dr. Hadley walked through an adjoining hallway to the waiting room. He was carrying a bag in his right hand as he rushed to the emergency room I was in. Mom and Dad were crushed knowing what was in that bag—my right arm.

It was tough for me, at the age of 9, hearing comments like, "He's probably not going to make it." My thoughts were that they must have been talking about someone else. I was very quiet and at this time, still not sure about how badly I was hurt.

The doctor on call in the emergency room that night was Dr. William Chleborad. He entered the emergency room and took charge. You could tell he was very respected. When he entered the emergency room, it was like he had a cape and a big "S" on his chest. All the support staff jumped at each of his commands.

His first goal was to stabilize my condition. Secondly, he wanted to patch up the shoulder where the arm used to be, and third, make a decision on the torn and mangled leg—if it could even be called that. The easy decision would have been to amputate the leg right below the knee. The tough decision was to try to save the leg and reconstruct it. Dr. Chleborad was amazed at the case before him.

The leg was a mangled mess. The tibia and fibula were broken. The fibula was crushed in a 3.5-inch segment. The muscles were torn and mangled. There was a strip of skin one-half inch wide on the back of my leg, along with a strip of muscle that was the only thing connecting my lower leg to my body.

Dr. Chleborad was an accomplished surgeon who had been practicing medicine for more than 13 years. He was also the father of six children. He had seen amputees and experienced many other interesting surgeries in his residency in the U.S. Air Force. To him, there was something about this 9-year-old little boy who was on the operating table that was both special and a challenge.

The two main arteries that leave the chest and go into the arm were restricted through the course of that day's events—no blood was pumping out of them, but they were pulsating and beating in rhythm with my heart. They had somehow cauterized on their own. Without this miracle, I would have pumped too much blood out of my body, ultimately taking my life.

Once again, another miracle.

The chest cavity was open and Dr. Chleborad was

amazed that the internal organs had not been damaged—or even fallen out of the open, exposed side of my body.

The surgery went on through the night. The first time I remember waking up, I opened my eyes and there were my mother and father wearing masks in a sterile room. I was in the intensive care unit. I was considered a "dirty" case because of all the grass, gravel, dirt and silage that was creating infection inside my body. The infection was intense and the battle with this infection was just beginning.

My family came into the room to see me. I couldn't see their faces or touch their hands because they had to be dressed in sterile gowns, masks and plastic gloves. They looked at me and had tears in their eyes. They were tired, scared, concerned and confused about the whole incident.

My father—or my mother, for that matter—would have changed places with me had they been able to.

Dad continued to feel guilty and responsible for the accident. The burden on his shoulders and the pain he was going through were much greater than mine. With true grit and determination, I could work through my pain. Dad had to deal with his pain and emotion in a different way.

Mom never left my bedside. The pain and anguish of a mother seeing her "baby" boy on the edge of death, minus one limb and another limb barely attached must have been intolerable. What must she be going through? But she never gave up. She stayed by my side, sleeping in a chair next to my bed each and every night—always there to love me, to hold my hand, rub my back and to support me. This gave me great comfort, just to know my Mom was always there, 24 hours a day, seven days a week.

I was scared and very weak. I did not have the energy to stay awake more than a few minutes at a time. The pain medication I was receiving made me very drowsy. I dozed off after each shot, which I received in the thigh. Each time I fell asleep in my first few days in the intensive care unit, my family didn't know if I was going to wake up again—I'd won a couple of battles to stay alive, but to escape the danger zone and win the war to keep my life was still days or weeks off.

The small community of Lyons suddenly came to life. A prayer vigil was started by the Methodist church. The doors of the church where our family had attended were open 24 hours a day. People from the area fell to their knees in prayer to ask God to spare my life, lift up and comfort my family and make the best of this tragic situation.

The synergy of love, selflessness and caring that sprung up out of the community of Lyons is a strong testimony of Small Town America. The battle lines were drawn, the community rallied to the front lines. The people stepped up in every way: Food was delivered to our home; chores were done on the farm; prayers, cards, letters and many other acts of kindness surrounded us.

Dad had approximately 100 calves in feedlots at the time. Neighbors stepped up and fed the cattle on a daily basis, and tended to the tasks of the day on our farm. Our friends truly took care of the day-to-day details so that my mother and father could stay with—and focus on—my recovery.

I had survived the immediate trauma and its consequences. But only days later, another huge, critical fight, the battle against pain and infection, was really getting cranked up.

I was experiencing excruciating pain in my shoulder. I could feel my right arm burning as if it were in a kettle of boiling water. The nurses asked me if I needed a pain shot and I always said yes. It seemed at times that there wasn't enough pain medication to ease the burning sensation.

The painkiller was an injection in my left thigh area. The

medication seemed to wear off after about 3½ hours. Then I asked Mom to call the nurse's station for another one. My life was now based on a four-hour window of pain medication. It was as if I had a time clock inside of me that went off each time I needed another shot.

I was heavily bandaged and knew my right arm had been injured. In my mind, I could feel my right fingers, I could move them, but my arm seemed so heavy, I thought it was in a cast or so heavily bandaged that I could not lift it.

Still, the shock was just beginning to wear off as I spent my second, third and fourth nights in the hospital.

Dr. Chleborad came in every morning to check on me. I was always his first stop. Doc was a serious man—always intense and loved to poke and prod medical tools in and at me and ask if it hurt. I really got sick of that. I always wondered what kind of answer he was really looking for.

He broke the news to me. "Ron, the tractor somehow ran over your arm and amputated it." I wasn't sure what "amputated" meant at the time, so I responded with a studious, "What?" He then explained that my right arm and shoulder were cut off by the tractor at the scene of the accident. I thought he was nuts. What kind of doctor would say that? I could physically feel the fingers on my right hand touching each other. I could feel pain in my right arm. Who was he trying to kid?

Doc went on to explain that the pain and feeling I had was called "phantom pain." Phantom pain is where the nerve endings still think the limb is still there, when in reality, it's not.

That was absolutely the worst pain I have ever experienced. There was simply no relief. The pain medication made me drowsy, and I slept for two or three hours when the pain woke me again. I could only get the pain shots every four hours. I could usually deal with the pain while I slept, but the next two or three hours were pure hell. When would this pain subside?

# 4

## Dealing With the Pain

The pain was excruciating. The whole family was experiencing it—my mom, dad, my brothers and myself. As I look back today, I was always in the best position of all of us. The pain I had to deal with was easy to handle compared to the rest of my family.

The pain and guilt my father was experiencing must have been tremendous...all the feelings of anger, confusion and responsibility for his 9-year-old son's accident.

Dad asked, "Why would God do this to our family? What type of God do we have? Why the Gustafson family? Why Ronnie? He was going to be the best athlete in the family. He had all the tools for stardom. Now what will come of his life? How will we handle this whole tragedy as a family?"

Dad went through a living hell. He blamed himself for the whole accident. "Why did I have Ronnie on the tractor with me? Why was he on the side of the tractor where the wheel came off? Why? Why!" This was the first time my mother had seen my father cry. The burden was so great.

People were assuring Dad that it was not his fault. He said, "You can say that, but I know I did it to my son. Every time I see him, I will know I did it to my little boy."

Mom was asking, "Was it a punishment due to my pride?" Only a week or so before the accident, Mom had stood in her bedroom as I came out of the bathroom and walked down the hallway into my room only wearing shorts. Mom watched me with great pride and thought, "What a perfect build!" She saw me as physically perfect for a 9-year-old. She saw me as a little boy with a great personality, intelligent, good-looking and multitalented. I had it all! Was God now taking my mother down because of this pride?

Our family had always struggled financially, with extended family issues and with the small family farm challenges. Now Mom and Dad were simply broken and pleading with God, "Please God! Please God! Please God!" As they waited at the hospital to see me, my mother and father gave up on the words to use to talk with God. They were physically, emotionally and mentally drained. It came to a point where they simply said, "We can't do it anymore God, it is up to you!"

**Following are the thoughts and recollections of my loving mother, Joyce Gustafson:**

"Ronnie and Dad were headed out to work that day. I remember Don coming to the door, carrying Ronnie, saying he was hurt, 'Ronnie's dead! Get help!' I didn't know what to think. I had just gotten off the phone with one of the older boys, and I had just hung up. I was still standing by the telephone. Don laid him down in the yard, and got his second wind, and went out and brought Ronnie into the house through the front door and put him on the floor. Ronnie looked at me and said, 'Mom, don't worry, I will be OK.' I could not believe it—Ronnie never cried, and yet he was only 9 years old. I called the rescue squad number, and it seemed to me to take forever. Of course, as it turned out, it wasn't that long. But I could not wait, so I called the operator and they patched it through. Jon Heideman, Dick Strehle and Lee Appleby—they were the three who went with us. Jon drove the ambulance. Dick and Lee rode in the back with

Ronnie, and I rode up front. We got to the emergency room in Fremont. Somebody in Lyons had called Dr. Kim, our Methodist minister. He walked into the emergency room right behind us as they were cutting Ron's clothes off of his leg and foot in the emergency room, and had everyone stop work for a minute, held hands and said a prayer—right there in the emergency room. That same day, a lady from the Assembly of God church, Marjorie Ayer—who wasn't even a member of our church—called the Methodist church and got a prayer vigil started for Ron, and the church stayed open through the night.

"At the hospital, everyone worked to clean up Ronnie. He was so dirty because he had been thrown into the dirt. Dad talked to Lee Appleby, and told him we had to start selling a lot of things we had, because it was obvious we had to get some funds from somewhere.

"Dr. Chleborad—we didn't know who he was before that—came in and just took charge. We of course didn't know what was going on, because we hadn't been in a hospital that much. But Dr. Chleborad came in and was in total control, and really knew what was going on, what to do, and that sort of thing. Through friends and neighbors, we were able to track down Ronnie's brothers. We had to tell them what had happened.

"Dr. Chleborad was talking about the condition of Ronnie's leg, that it was a mess. Dad said, 'Doc, you have to save my boy's leg—you just have to save it.' He said, 'Don, I'll do what I can. I promise you that.'"

"When the rescue squad left, they showed Dr. Hadley where the accident had been. Dr. Hadley picked up Ronnie's arm up off the road. He had it wrapped in the sheets. He picked up the arm and brought it to the hospital, but it was not going to be able to be reattached or anything. So they had to dispose of the arm at the hospital.

"They also went back and got Ronnie's shoes—those were his favorite shoes. They had belonged to 'Old Faithful' Johnson, the man who we rented the land from. They were high top, lace up work boots.

"After Ron had been in intensive care for four days, they took him out to listen to the Nebraska football game—they didn't allow radios in the intensive care. At that point, Ron's brothers were in his room with him, playing board games with him. One of the nurses' aides, an elderly woman, came out of his room and found me. She was angry. She said, 'Those boys won't even let their little brother win one game!' But that's how they were. They made Ronnie earn everything.

"Ron had surgery every two or three days after that—I honestly lost track of how many. When they did skin grafting on Ronnie's right shoulder, they took skin from his stomach and right thigh. Ronnie said that after that his stomach and thigh hurt worse than the shoulder itself. I guess one thing that sticks out in my mind is when Doc Chleborad came out of the emergency room that first day. He said that the arteries in Ronnie's arm had miraculously closed off, saving his life. And he couldn't believe the good fortune that Don had paid attention to the lower part of Ronnie's leg, because it was so close to amputation that everything had to work out perfectly to save it, and it did work out. Doc Chleborad said, 'There was someone bigger than all of us in that room today.' He meant God, that He was watching over Ronnie.

"Jerry Mathers, Ronnie's fourth-grade teacher, was there from start to finish for Ronnie. If Mr. Mathers could not get down to the hospital, he would still call. He also had Ronnie's classmates come down or call, or write letters. We were just so blessed. I knew the Lord would get Ronnie through this. And all of his friends, our neighbors, Ronnie's brothers and people like Mr. Mathers were a gift from God who helped Ronnie—and all of us—through this.

"Our insurance for Ronnie was capped at $10,000, so that ran out four days after the accident. People from all over—many of whom we didn't know or barely knew—started donating money to the fund set up at the Lyons bank."

"We wanted Ron to have a normal life. His Dad was

always thinking of ways to customize things for Ron, so he would always feel like he was just another kid. He devised a way for Ron to open a storm window by himself, using a wire to twist which would unlatch the window. He hung the mattress and tire for Ron to practice throwing. For as proud as I was of Ronnie, I was also proud of his father."

My mother also was in the process of making a huge sacrifice. As a teacher in Bancroft, she signed her paycheck over EVERY single time for 10 years to pay my medical bills. Imagine that: Going a whole decade and not taking home a dime for all of her hard work educating young people. My mother is a role model as a mother, teacher and human being. She is always working behind the scenes to take care of her family. Like my father, she is a beacon of courage that I can only hope to emulate.

**Following are the thoughts of my father, Don Gustafson:**
"I kept praying Ronnie was going to live. I did not want him to lose his leg—losing the arm was bad enough, but to lose the leg too would be too much.

"The accident was something that did not have to happen, but it did. Of course I blamed myself—who else was there to blame? It should have been me instead of Ronnie. I kept asking myself, 'Why couldn't it have been me?' I have spent over 25 years trying to put the vivid images of that day behind me. It hurts so much to revisit the horror."

Dr. Chleborad was also a spiritual warrior: He did many of my treatments on his own time, not accepting any payment from us. We still had to cover the hospital bills, but Dr. Chleborad donated much of his time for me. He was truly a skilled, compassionate physician.

My brothers had to deal with the pain of finding out that their little brother had been severely injured in a farm accident.

My brother Rick was just starting his sophomore year at Midland Lutheran College in Fremont, Nebraska. His version follows:

**Following are the thoughts and recollections of my oldest brother, Rick Gustafson:**

"I would call home collect as usual, visit with Mom and Dad and see if Dad needed any help with corn-picking or anything in general. I was visiting with Mom in the late afternoon. She said Jim was at football practice and that Ron was helping Dad with the chores and were on their way to the east farm. Everything was normal, there wasn't any deviation from the day-to-day happenings. Ron, Jim, Mike and I had always helped with the chores, the field work and thought nothing of it. A few minutes later, Mom said she would call me back because she heard dad yelling.

"Being the studious scholar that I was in those days, I was in a friend's room studying in a beanbag chair. I was called to the phone on the floor of Gunderson Hall. The dorm had only one phone per floor so anyone close would answer it. When I answered the call, it was Jon Heideman who was very somber and told me that there had been a serious accident with a family member and asked if I had a way to get to the hospital. I did not ask who it was, or what happened, I just went across town to the hospital. He said that he would meet me there. The Dodge County Memorial Hospital is not far from Midland's campus and I arrived in just a few minutes. Jon met me at the emergency entrance and said my little brother had been seriously injured. I just kept going until I found Mom and Dad. They were in a small room just off the emergency room area. Mom was crying. She met me and hugged me and told me Ron had lost his arm, maybe his leg and might even lose his life. Dad was shaking and smoking three times as fast as usual. I was scared, crying and asking Mom if it was really that bad. 'Was Ron going to die? Could they reattach the arm? How did the accident happen?' I was told some of what happened, but not everything. What did Ron do? He did not deserve this! There were a lot of questions that I was asking, but wasn't getting any answers. There was a guy with a ponytail who was asking Mom and Dad questions. As it turns out it was his job to collect information, consent forms, and medical history before surgery and admittance. I asked where Ron was. I was told he was in one of the ER rooms where he was being prepped and cleaned up for surgery. Mom and Dad were able to see Ron. I was too scared to go in to see him and scared that he might die. Talk about being paralyzed. It was not that much longer when Ron was wheeled out of the room and proceeded to surgery.

"I don't remember when Jim arrived from football practice or how he got there, but I remember sitting with Mom, Dad, and Jim in a surgical waiting room. It was hot and very small. The wait seemed like time had stopped. It was during this time that Mom told us what happened. Ron made it through surgery and was placed in the intensive care unit. We then met Dr. Chleborad who told us about Ron's status, what had taken place in surgery that evening and that there would be several more surgeries to come. He said he didn't know if they would be able to save Ron's leg at that time. He said that his arteries and vessels were larger than kids' his age and that this is what would save his leg. Ron's cardiovascular development was probably aided by the fact he would run one to two miles with Mike followed by sprints while Mike was training for football.

"There was a policy in place in the intensive care unit that only so many visitors could see the patient and for only a limited time period. For Ron, that rule got stretched big time! The next day we were all trying to adapt, to be strong for Ron. As it turns out he was the one who kept our spirits up. There were definitely rough times, though. One time, Ron asked for a drink and said he had the glass in his right hand. He really didn't. He was experiencing the phantom pains and only thought he had the glass in his hand. I also remember Ron coining my nickname in the intensive care unit that has stuck for years, Dickie-bird! I'll get him for that someday!

"I also remember when the Nebraska Cornhuskers were playing a football game and the radio announcer, Lyle Bremmser, talked about Ron's accident and wished Ron a speedy recovery. Ron's eyes perked up and he said, 'That's me!'

"I wanted to quit playing basketball my sophomore year, but Ron encouraged me—somehow convinced me—into continuing my college career. He always had a great attitude. There were a lot of surgeries, phantom pains, bed sores, and back rubs he always took full advantage of, and long hours at the hospital. I always spent as much time as I could at the hospital to ensure that Ron was OK."

**Following are the thoughts and recollections of my older brother, Mike Gustafson:**

"In the fall of 1975 I was a freshman at Augustana College in Sioux Falls, South Dakota. I was one of the 22 freshmen on the football team for the Augustana Vikings. We had finished practice for the day and had made it back for dinner at the college commons, just in time before they shut down the dinner line for the night.

"After dinner, about a half dozen of us stopped by Dean Johnson's room to talk about college life and how each of us should be in a starting position on the team instead of on the scout squad. Dean's room was a normal gathering place for most of us as it was on the first floor of the dorm and the second room on the left as you entered from the north side door. For some reason, we did not use the spacious main floor entry into the freshman dorm very much....probably because it was what we were supposed to do.

"The phone rang on Dean's desk. Dean answered the phone and his look of concern was directed right at me. He handed me the phone and without much issue I answered with "hello." I cannot remember who it was on the other end of the phone, but I was told that Bill Brunton was on his way to Sioux Falls to get me as my brother Ron was in an accident. I asked him how serious it was and how it happened. I was unable to get any information that could give me an idea on why Bill Brunton was driving the 112 miles from Lyons to the Augustana campus. For some reason my folks did not want me to drive home alone.

"After hanging up, I told the guys what I knew of the situation and that one of my parents' friends was going to pick me up at the lobby of the dorm. I wasn't sure when I would be back or what exactly was going on, but I had a bad feeling that it was not good. To my amazement, several of my closest friends verbalized their responsibilities regarding my absence from the team and also from school.

"I was feeling somewhat dazed and unbalanced. While Bill Brunton was a close friend to my parents, my relationship was clearly from a distance and would not compel him to drive to Sioux Falls in the dark. I could not connect anything that was happening, but maybe Bill would help me sort things out when he arrived.

"Dean's voice brought me back to the room as he was on the phone talking with Pastor Pete, the defensive line coach of the team. Pastor Pete's responsibilities doubled as football coach and campus pastoral staff. Dean was informing Pastor Pete of my situation, vague as it was, and would Pastor Pete notify the head coach and help with any professors on campus who were involved in my classes.

"Frank, his real name was Don Peterson but Frank was his chosen name, was trying to coax out my class schedule so Pastor Pete could cover for me with my professors. I believed I babbled my schedule as Frank stopped his persistence.

"Next I remember my bag was packed and I was sitting in the lobby of the dorm waiting for Bill's arrival. I began to think: What had Chopper done this time? Did he swallow poison? No, Jim had done that years ago...and he lived. Did he step, or maybe sit on a nail and everyone was fussing over him? No, Jim had done that years ago, too...and once again he lived. What had that little turkey done to mess up my college schedule, I thought, and why did I feel like crying?

"How did they find me in Dean's room to get me the call? Why was everyone so persistent in this thing? What is going on? And Bill, I thought to myself, better have some answers."

"An hour or so passed as I waited, thought, said hello to friends passing by and watched two freshmen perfect their skills at the foosball table located in the lounge area of the first floor. I recognized Bill immediately as he entered the dorm. His smile was a fake. We exchanged hellos and walked directly to the car. The two-and-a-half-hour car ride to Fremont passed very quickly. The expected answers from Bill never came. Each time I asked him about the situation and Ron's accident, he stonewalled me. He either didn't have the words or didn't want to lie, he just looked out of the driver's side window and told me to talk with my parents who would be at the hospital when we arrived.

"Have you ever visited a friend at the hospital who had just had routine surgery? You know, the kind where there wasn't any risk to their health, but was just something that needed to be done? You are making the visit as a friend and to hopefully get them through the boring day or so of their hospital stay. You don't quite feel good about going into the hospital, but you look forward to clowning around for a while, joking it up. Well, that was the feeling I had walking into the Fremont Hospital. You know, the mentality that says, 'Let's go tell Chopper to suck it up and go home so we can get some sleep.'

"I was not prepared for the next 20 minutes and I have never recovered from the crash of our universe, as I regarded it. The elevator ride to the emergency floor took forever. The doors opened and there was a big guy in the opening of the doors keeping me from leaving the elevator. Good grief, I thought, 'Can't this guy move it so I can find Chopper and see what all the fuss is about?'

"Then, a large man appeared. 'We did it up this time, Mike...' he said.

"The big guy in the doorway was my dad. I could now

focus a little to make out his features. He was unshaven, tired looking, and slouching at the shoulders. My dad never slouched. Mom stood behind him and a little to his right. She was crying and her lower face was covered with her hands.

I could not take not knowing what's going on. I asked, 'Where's Chopper?'

"My next recollection was standing in Chopper's critical care room. He was covered with tubes, bags of clear goop, stainless steel poles held monitors, and other equipment I was amazed could fit into the small room. However, what caught my eye was a device out of his leg that looked like a stainless steel vice grip. What possible could he have done to his leg to require this device? If it was broken it must be pretty bad.

"Ron was lying on his back with his head turned away from the door entry to the room. He was asleep, but it looked like a painful sleep. I noticed bandages on his right shoulder and wondered how bad this was if his leg was banged up and his shoulder was hurt as well. His left arm was lying at his side and it was scratched up and appeared to be in bad shape. What had happened to him?

"Once outside the room, I asked Mom and Dad when the bandages were coming off his right shoulder and if his right arm or leg was the worst. Mom gave me a complete blank stare. Then she said, 'Mike, Ron's right arm has been cut off.'

"The feeling that came over me at that point can only be described with a quick reference to the farm life. Hot wires erected to keep cattle in fields as a farm boy had zapped me. These single stranded barbed wire fences were temporary and usually were set up to allow cattle to graze in areas for a short period of time while keeping them away from areas not intended for their pleasure. To make the fence effective, a small electric current pulsed through the wire. Once touched by a cow, it became grounded, the circuit was complete, and a shock was sent through its body. The shock wasn't harmful, but was incredibly painful for a short period of time and trained her to stay away from the area. As a boy, this form of zapping was funny to watch when it happened to a cow. It was quite different, when it happened to you when not paying attention. The circuit would arch in your teeth between your fillings, in your joints and give you a moment when you couldn't see. And if the grass was wet and the juice was really flowing, it would cause you to exhale and lose your breath. In the coming moments, I was about to get 'zapped.'

"My mother continued, 'Don't you know? His arm was lost in the tractor accident.'

"I looked at Dad, and then I got zapped. I felt like I had been frozen in time. I stood there with nothing to say or do! I went back in the Chopper's room. I was numb. I leaned over him in his bed and pulled the sheets up under his chin. As I pulled the sheets back to pull them up, I caught my first look at Chopper's right side, where his right arm used to be. I broke down by the side of his bed and cried, then I got so mad I hit a wall with my fist. Why did God do this to my little brother? He had trained with me as I was preparing for my freshman year of football at Augustana. He ran with me every day, he did sit-ups and push-ups with me. We did chores in the early mornings together before we went to school. We were so much alike as brothers and competitors. He was so good at everything he did. Now what? How was he going to live?

"It is strange how the human mind digests information. But this time, my mind did not digest the information, as the shock was too much. How could Chopper's arm be gone? How could my little brother have gone through something this horrendous? I could feel the electricity arch through my mouth, my joints felt the shock and I thought I had fallen down, but I was leaning against the wall of the hallway. 'You didn't know?' Mom asked. 'We thought you knew.'

"Every bone, every fiber within me cried denial at the news. I couldn't put it all together. It didn't make sense. The thoughts raced through my mind: 'Was he going to die? I saw his arm. It couldn't be gone! I will not accept this! I demand to be told it is a lie! Who's responsible here? I will not allow this to happen!'

"My father came over to me. 'Sit down Mike, I want to fill you in on what happened.' Dad didn't look too good but he wanted to talk about it, but I was having problems understanding spoken words, the unspoken feelings were too loud. Rick sat in a chair in the lobby, looking at the floor, I remember feeling Jim's presence, but I can't place him in the room.

"Dad told me about what happened that day...The road where Ron's arm was lost was the same road that provided the path to endless hours of running just a few months ago, for both Ron and me. I was in training for my first year of college football. He was mimicking my every move. Mile after mile I ran on that road to develop the endurance to make it through three-times-a-day college football practices. At 8 years of age, he couldn't match the pace of my runs, but he exceeded my will. He never gave up, he never gave in to the heat or the dust we both chewed on that dirt road. After running, we would stretch, and then push-ups and sit-ups. I was determined to make it in college and Ron was just as determined.

"As we waited in the room, someone from the hospital appeared in front of my father.

"My father told this man, 'I think I just killed my son.'

"My mother looked at him and said, 'No Don, you can't think like that, you saved him, you made sure that you got him here, for help.'

"Mom was ensuring that Dad stayed with us. I had never seen my Dad look so alone. Critical times in the life of a family can either be the flame of destruction or the fusion of determination. I experienced and witnessed the fusion of my parent's will that would be the basis of the survival for the family and their marriage. Those supportive words of love from Mom to Dad would be the beginning of the rebuilding of their family. Unknown to anyone in that room at that time, a marriage could have been shattered by faulty words that could never be called back. But through either the grace of God or the determination of our parents, or both, the first 24 hours after the accident proved to be powerful and that power would need to be drawn upon many times over the next two years."

**Jim, another older brother, was at football practice at Lyons High School. Here is his recollection:**
"I heard the sirens from the practice field. I thought to myself, 'I wonder who got hurt?' Needless to say, I would soon find out it was Ron. I left practice and as I was walking out to my car, Mrs. Regina Heideman came up to me and said that Mom had to leave town for a bit and that I was supposed to come with her. I went to her home for about 30 minutes and I remember the whole time I was there that something was wrong, but as always I did not question it. Then Mr. Elton Southwell, who was the father of one of my teammates' and a neighbor, came and picked me up and took me to his house and said there had been an accident and Ron was involved.

"After leaving their house, to this day I still don't know why we went there, we were driving to Fremont to the hospital and I just knew that Ron had been bitten by the hogs. I thought he probably had tripped over the hot wire fence and the hogs went after him.

"When we arrived at the hospital, I met Dad and he said that he might have killed Ron in an accident. I could not talk. I remember sitting in the emergency room with my head down crying and wishing it were me. When I went to the room and saw Ron all beat up, I couldn't believe what had happened. How could God do this to Ron?"

My brother Mike had the toughest time dealing with the scene, yet the pain for my entire family was excruciating. Each member of the family tried to take on responsibility and give themselves up for me with acts of kindness and encouragement. Each of them wished they were the one in my position. Each wanted to be the sacrificial lamb.

The staff of the Dodge County Memorial Hospital was incredible. They helped our whole family deal with the crisis. Nurses and nurses aides gathered in my room whenever there was a break and played games, read the mail to me, and decorated my room with cards by attaching hundreds of them to the wall. They also loved to watch the TV show "Happy Days" with me.

One would have thought I had my own entourage of medical staff. At times there were seven or eight of them in my room. I was typically heavily drugged with medication and crept in and out of conversations.

My family built great relationships with the greatest team of caregivers ever. These relationships with the medical staff continue on today.

We received letters of encouragement from all over the country. People who had read about or heard about the accident wanted to encourage and pray for us.

*"Enclosed please find a check to be added to Ronnie's fund. His story was such a beautiful testimony of faith—both his and his family's—that it will, no doubt, influence far more people than they'll ever imagine by giving them the incentive they need to look to prayer for help and then 'tough it out.' In these days of so much negative thinking it is such a thrill to read about someone with a good positive approach to life and doubly so when that person is of such a young age. May God continue to bless each one of this family today and in the days ahead."*
*Gwen M.*

Our family was embraced with prayers, love, kindness and the challenge of healing in the future.

I continued to recover and become stronger. Surgery after

surgery, pain shot after pain shot, I was on the road to recovery. It seemed like a long dusty, lonely road. Even though my family was always there for me, I seemed to be alone. Maybe it was the minute-to-minute battle with phantom pains or maybe it was my unknown future. It may have been the guilt that I felt being the center of attention and watching my family give up all they had for me.

Mom continued to care for me at my bedside. I felt so helpless. The embarrassment was great as well. I was a proud, strong, determined little boy. Now I found myself laying naked in a bed and having nurses and my Mom bathing me daily. I was introduced to bedpans, urinals and catheters. I was so dependent upon other people now, for everything.

A nurse came into my room every four hours to take my blood pressure and temperature. I would have given anything to have a full night of undisturbed rest. I kept thinking that this had to be a bad dream. I will wake up any minute. I just wanted to go home and play on the farm.

I spent 24 hours a day on my back since I couldn't roll over or be on my side. The sweat and irritation on my back developed bedsores. These blisters burned and made every move uncomfortable. It seemed as though I couldn't get enough lotion rubbed onto my back to ease the burning sensation. Mom spent countless hours trying to make me comfortable.

Meals were delivered to my hospital room and Mom opened the milk carton, put extra ketchup on my hamburger and assisted in feeding me. Using my left hand to feed myself was one of the first big adjustments. Soup, Jell-O and other fine foods became a horrendous task to get on a spoon and up to my mouth. There were tears of frustration when it spilled down my chest and tears of joy when I finally met and beat the challenge.

The pain medication became the last obstacle I had to overcome before being released from the hospital. I was addicted and had to break it before going home.

I had become a 9-year-old junkie craving the need for the next "hit." The doctors devised a plan of using a placebo without my knowledge. They thought that the shot was all in my head now. They filled my syringe with a saline solution instead of the medication. They gave me the injection and it burned as it went in, just like the real thing. This time the pain did not subside. I went ballistic and began hitting nurses, biting and fighting.

The medical staff had to restrain me and tied me to the bed with straps. I went through the painful process of withdrawal in a two-day period. My family struggled through the time with me, but we made it.

After some 42 days, I was released from the hospital and looked forward to being at home and seeing the great outdoors again. I longed for the fresh country air in northeast Nebraska.

# 5

## The Ultimate Cruising Vessel

I was finally released from the hospital after a six-week stay and 18 reconstructive surgeries. I was too weak to sit up in a car for the ride from Fremont back home to Lyons, so my father bought the ultimate cruising vessel, a 1974 Chevrolet station wagon. This car was a beauty; green with wood-grain paneling. I asked Dad if he was going to take it out of the crate. He didn't think that was funny at all. There was a luggage rack on top and Dad customized the beast by cutting a piece of plywood that slid in the back of the station wagon. Dad folded the two bench-type seats down in the back of the car and slide the plywood into the back. He then bought a twin-sized mattress to put on top of it. This created a slide out bed and a ride that seemed to me to be fit for royalty.

The nurses wheeled me out to the patient loading area. Dad, a very proud station wagon owner, pulled up to the door. He opened the back of the vehicle and pulled the plywood with the mattress out of the back. He propped the plywood up on a stand and then gently picked me up out of the wheelchair.

He approached me from the left side and placed his left hand under my legs and placed my right calf, which had a splint on it, in his left hand. He wrapped his right arm around my waist and lifted me out of the wheelchair. I wrapped my left arm around his shoulders and neck and hung on as best I could as he carefully walked over to the mattress and laid me down on it.

Dad slid the mattress back into the car. My head would be toward the front of the car just behind the front seat. He started the car and headed for home.

The ride was uneventful. I slept most of the way. I remember as we approached the intersection where we turned off Highway 77 and headed to our farm that I had a very anxious feeling in my stomach. We turned onto the hilly gravel road that leads to our farm. As we went over the last hill on the approach to our driveway, this anxious feeling turned into excitement to see the cattle lined up at the manger in the feed lots, our dog Bubba, and to be in the great outdoors again.

Dad backed the station wagon up to the back door. He put it in park, opened the back door and window and slid the plywood/mattress out. It was a cool day in October and the beauty of the farm and the fresh air was the most healing thing I had had for weeks.

What a relief to be home...what a relief to be alive.

Dad's strong arms picked me up off the mattress. This was the first of thousands of lifts that he made over the next year. He carried me into the house and set me in my bed. I was tired and weak from the trip and rested most of the day.

Having been in the hospital for six weeks, the house seemed foreign to me. The rooms seemed smaller, the lights dimmer but the amount of love was even greater.

Mom and Dad went out of their way to serve me—what a wonderful Christian testimony of love and servanthood. They worked extraordinarily hard to meet my needs. They jumped at every beck and call to bring food and drink to my fingertips.

I was extremely skinny, frail and weak beyond anything I could have ever comprehended. All the tone, muscle, strength and life in my body had been zapped. I was helpless from a personal perspective, but tenaciously strong from a family point of view.

Dad was incredible. He carried me everywhere I went. The station wagon was designed for the long over-the-road hauls, while Dad was used for the short over-the-sidewalk hauls.

The green machine was fast becoming the road burner between our farm in Lyons and the Dodge County Memorial Hospital in Fremont. Every other day, Dad got up early, did the farm chores, loaded me into the car and drove me to Fremont to see Dr. Chleborad to have the dressings on my leg changed or to have more surgeries. They put me to sleep each time because of the pain and the nature of the procedures.

Going into the operating room was old hat for me. The nurses stripped me down, threw on one of those "rear-vented" gowns and talked with me through the entire ritual leading up to the surgery. I could never see their faces because of the masks they wore, but always trusted the beautiful eyes and warm voices that came from behind the masks that were making me feel so safe and secure. They were always encouraging.

To a 9-year-old little boy, the operating room was very intimidating. The lights were bright, the walls sterile, and it always seemed to be very cool. The staff moved me onto the table and I stared up at the bright surgical lights above me. Nurses were always laying out instruments for the doctor and talking with me as they worked intently. The operating rooms seemed to have more hardware than our local hardware store. They had their own inventory of hammers, drills and screwdrivers.

The anesthesiologist came in and stood awkwardly on the left side of the table. Typically they would have the intravenous tubing in the patient's right arm, in my case, they had trouble using my right arm for obvious reasons. The room was not set up for doctors to work on the left side of the table. They had to move some stands and equipment so he could get close to me and hook the drugs up to the IV.

The anesthesiologist asked me to begin to count to 20 and I got to six or seven and I was fast asleep. The feeling was eerie. It seemed that I was floating into never-never land.

I woke up an hour or so later in the recovery room where the nurse, who must have been hard of hearing, would be talking to me in a very loud voice. "Ron. Ron. Ron—can you hear me?" If I hadn't been so tired, I would have yelled back at her. Of course I could hear her. The whole hospital could!

Doc came in and wheeled me out after the drugs wore off. We always stopped by the nurses' lounge and picked up a couple of cookies for the long ride in the wheelchair down the hallway. The nurses all yelled at Doc and me for stealing their cookies. It got to be a great game that we all played. As busy as Doc was, he always took the time to wheel me out to my parents and fill them in on the progress.

On one of our trips to Fremont for the dressing change, Doc asked me if I was ready to go through the procedure without being put to sleep. I said sure. I was very nervous and wasn't sure what to expect. They wheeled me into the operating room to start the procedure.

They began to cut the elastic wrap that held the plaster splint to my leg. This splint started at the tip of my toes, ran down my foot, curved around my heel and ran the length of my leg up to my upper thigh. It wrapped halfway around my leg like a cup. The shin area was heavily bandaged with gauze and padded for protection and absorption of the blood and infectious drainage.

The dirty nature of the accident had created infection and osteomyelitis, a rotting of the bone. The skin grafting had trouble growing because of the drainage from two holes in the shin area that exposed the bone.

The process of peeling the bandages away was painful and made me very tense. Doc finished taking the bandages off and asked if I were ready to see my leg.

I was nervous. It had been approximately two months since I had seen my leg. At that time it was a normal, strong, athletic leg, full of life, spring and athleticism.

The team of nurses supported the leg with their hands under the calf and thigh area and slowly lifted the leg as I lay on my back. I rolled my eyes down toward the leg and saw a skinny, disfigured, area called the shin and a foot that was missing two toes. That moment has been fixed in my mind to this day. I could not say a word. I just stared at it and began to cry. This was one of the first reality checks I had in seeing the real damage that had been done. This was the first moment I realized I was really injured, badly.

How would I ever walk on that thing I just saw? My dream of playing professional football was dead. I was in denial. My leg was gross. It was deformed. There was no muscle. I could see the bone through a hole in my shin. What would other people say when they saw it if I couldn't stand the sight of it?

I could only remember telling myself that I had to be strong for Mom and Dad. I couldn't show the emotion of what had just taken place. My parents had been through so much. I couldn't let them see the pain that I just experienced in seeing my leg. Surely I could hide it from them.

The nurses put the dressings on the leg again and our

typical fun and excitement as Doc wheeled me out seemed to be gone this time. Reality had set in and I was scared and ashamed of what was under all the dressings. There were no more secrets.

The trip back to the farm was very long and quiet as I dealt with the lasting image of what my leg looked like. I kept asking myself, "Was that really MY leg?"

The routine trips back to the hospital dwindled as my parents took on the responsibility of changing the dressings. Dad lifted me out of the bed and took the splint off while leaving the bloody bandages on my leg. He carried me to the bathroom and set me down in the warm bath water that Mom had run for me. I soaked in the water for a few minutes and the bandages softened up and peeled away from my skin.

I peeled the last bandage off and stared. The damage was tremendous and there was a hole the size of a half-dollar right on top. The drainage flowed out of this hole. Bits and pieces of dead bone also floated out. At first this scared me, then it became second nature to pull bone chips out of this hole. It became an adventure each night.

Doc had tried to put in a plate with screws to line up the bones to allow them to heal. One night while in the bathtub, I reached down and saw a screw. Curiosity got the best of me and I reached down to my shin area and grabbed the screw and pulled it out. The bone was rotting and the osteomyelitis was still at work. All the screws fell out. Dad always said I had a screw loose...

Eventually Doc had to perform another surgery and take strips of bone out of my hip and graft them into the shin area. I now have one bone from just below my knee to just above my ankle. This bone grafted together is supposed to be stronger than the individual bones side by side.

# 6

## How Would the People Around Me React?

The support from the people in Lyons was tremendous. The community raised funds for me and supported me with cards, notes and love.

My family was also very supportive. After I got home from the hospital, Dad bought a golf cart for me so I could be outside with him and get around the farm. My life did not come to an end; in essence it was a new start with a whole new set of challenges, both physical and emotional.

I started driving the golf cart all over the farm. It gave me great freedom to move about without Dad having to carry me. I felt in control and simply drove all over the farm. The snow began to fly and this created a new and exciting challenge for me. I could fishtail and spin out on the ice and snow as I drove around. I had a need for speed and power. My brothers were home for Christmas and I recall chasing them with the golf cart. They were all very fast and agile and were able to maneuver out of the way of my torpedo golf cart most of the time. I began to chase Jim down the driveway one time and he tried to lunge to a side. He was on snow and he slipped as he lost his footing. He was lying on the driveway. I was headed for him, full steam ahead. I truly tried to turn to miss him, but the front wheels slid and I kept moving straight for him at Mach speed. I ran over his ankle and for some reason he was mad. I finally came to a stop and turned around to see how badly I had hurt him. His face was red and I thought he was going to kill me. I stomped on the gas pedal and high-tailed it out of there.

Jim stood up and began to chase me. He fell because of the pain in his ankle and I didn't come back to the house until I was almost out of gas. Luckily, he had cooled off after an hour and didn't hurt me too badly.

There were many adventures on the golf cart. Dad forgot to tell me it wasn't a four-wheel drive golf cart. His oversight caused me to find more snowdrifts than I care to remember. There was more than one instance when I got stuck in the field and had to crawl out of the golf cart, sit on the ground with my right leg stiff in a splint and crawl home, many times over a quarter of a mile. I was cold and tired and Mom would look out the window and across the driveway and see me crawling to the house. She had to send Dad out to carry me the rest of the way. I guess they don't build a four-wheel drive golf cart that could meet the rugged, snowy terrain of our farm.

My first day back to school was scary. How would my old football buddies accept me? What would the girls say to me? How do I catch up on the two months of school that I had missed?

My parents and Mr. Mathers worked on the master plan to get me integrated into school once again. Dad took a padded chair and a footstool from our basement and moved it into my classroom. Dad loaded me up in the back of the station wagon and drove up to the front of the school. He slid the mattress out of the back, picked me up, carried me up the flight of stairs, opened the classroom door and carried me in. The entire class stood up and began to clap. Part of me was excited and part of me was embarrassed. Here I was a 9-year-old boy who used to be so strong and athletic, now being carried like a child into a fourth-grade classroom by his dad.

Dad set me down in the chair and propped my leg up on the footstool. The class continued to clap and began to gather around me. Dad left and I was on my own again. I was scared and did not know what to say or do. It sure felt good to be around my friends, though. It seemed like I had been gone for years. Everything felt so foreign.

I only lasted a couple of hours the first few weeks. Over time, my strength and stamina built up to the point where I could stay all day.

Math class was in the afternoon and I had missed so much. I had learned my multiplication tables pretty well, but the rest of my class had started doing long division while I was in the hospital. My classmates were weeks ahead of me. Mr. Mathers put 10 division problems on the chalkboard and the class began to work. I had no idea how to even begin. I felt very lonely and a tear began to creep into the corner of my eye. Should I ask for help? Would they laugh at me? Was I dumb?

It was a very lonely position. I had no where to turn. I didn't know how to take the first step to take action. I was simply frozen in fear and on the verge of humiliation.

Was this going to be the new me? Not knowing how to do anything? Afraid and nowhere to turn?

Jeff Burmester, who was a great buddy of mine who was always very helpful, came over to me when he was done with his problems and began to explain how to do the division problems. What a great feeling for me! Jeff went out of his way to kneel down beside my chair and help me out. To this day, it remains a moment I will never forget. It was just so neat—all the people who were put into my life along the way to help me when I struggled and was seemingly down and out. There was always someone there to help me or push me to the next level, which helped shape my personality and desire to help and assist others in their struggles.

As time went on, my strength increased. I began to hop on one foot to get around home and the classroom. Mr. Mathers stayed in the classroom with me during the lunch hour. I brought a rubber ball to school one day. It was about the size of a tennis ball. I sat in my chair and bet Mr. Mathers a soft drink that I could shoot the ball from my chair into the big metal trash can by his desk. He accepted the bet and lost his first cola to me. The first of many.

This was the beginning of some of the more fierce competitions in my life. We began to play H-O-R-S-E during recess and lunch hour. I took a shot. If I made it, Mr. Mathers would have to make the same shot or get a letter until the word "horse" was spelled out. I developed a desire for the game and started to shoot trick shots. Some of the shots included bouncing off the floor, banking against a wall and into the trash can. Other shots went off of the floor, banked against the two walls in the corner of the classroom and into the trash can. We got to be pretty good and had to call the shot before shooting.

My buddies flipped a coin for the chance to stay in the classroom with me to play H-O-R-S-E. We rebuilt our relationship. And my friends' fear of being around a one-armed guy seemed to dissipate. The love of competition seemed to draw us closer together and allow great friendships to be established. All of a sudden, winning became more important than worrying about what to say, or how to say something to their one-armed classmate.

I was encouraged and challenged at every corner.

**From the Lyons Mirror Sun**
Jim's Jumble
(Oct. 23, 1975)

This week's column is dedicated to Ronnie Gustafson.

If there were ever a more courageous and inspirational young man, we would certainly like to meet him.

We would say that if the courage displayed by this young man, after these past six weeks hasn't brought a tear or two to your eyes, nothing probably will.

Ronnie's spirits constantly remained high following the accident. Even in the ambulance on the way to the hospital he talked about how he would still be able to participate in sports, which is such a big part of his young life. And he has not changed that goal one bit.

And do you know he has made believers out of everyone?

We really believe that someday Ronnie will again be active in school sports just like his classmates.

It sometimes takes an accident like Ronnie's to make the rest of us re-evaluate our goals and outlook on life.

The good Lord works in mysterious ways, and everyone who has been touched in anyway by Ronnie's courageous spirit is the better for it.

In commenting on Mrs. Gustafson's statement of the Gustafson's wanting to thank everyone for their prayers, I would like to turn her statement around and thank the Gustafson family for their display of courage and faith.

But most of all, a great big thank you to Ronnie for his continuing high spirits. It has been an inspiration for all of us.

Ronnie, you are quite a young man. May God continue to bless you. Remember, no matter what lies ahead for you, just keep the faith.

# 7

## Sustenance Through Sports

Dad picked me up from school everyday and took me home in the ultimate cruising vessel. He took me out of the car and put me on the golf cart so I could drive around the farm with him so I knew what he was doing. I love watching Dad work.

At the end of the day I pulled up onto the driveway and Dad would throw the basketball to me. I caught the ball with my left hand, balanced the ball in the shooting position and shot the ball toward the basket. My hand was small and the ball seemed so big. The ball usually rolled off my hand to the left or the right as I started to launch it to the basket. It was extremely difficult to learn how to shoot with my left hand after being right-handed for nine years of my life.

A revolving cycle of frustration seemed to be evident in my life. Every time I turned around, I had to re-learn something. Each episode generated frustration, anger, fear but eventually hope. I never asked, "Why me?" As I looked at my family that was helping me so much I simply asked "Why not me?"

Dad always retrieved the ball and threw it back to me. I tried the same motion repeatedly. Finally the ball left my hand with just the right trajectory and went in the hoop. Now that was a rush! The electricity between Dad and me on that first basket was enough to light up a major city for a week. Dad and I were high-fiving and then he ran in to tell Mom. She came out and wanted to see another one in the hoop. We kept shooting until we got another one then another one, and with time and practice, made baskets became the norm.

The cold winter weather moved our basketball game into the garage where we worked on passing and began to throw the baseball. Dad barehanded my throw and walked the ball over to me, then I threw again. Eventually I put a baseball glove on my left hand and Dad threw the ball to me. Catching was a piece of cake. It was the same as I had done before the accident. I was now faced with getting the ball out of my glove and throwing it back to Dad. The early attempts were simple. I laid the glove in my lap, pulled my hand out of it, pulled the ball out of the glove and threw it to Dad. This process was very slow and I wanted to get faster. I did not want Dad to have to wait so long for me to throw the ball back to him.

In bed at night I tried a few different ideas. Nothing seemed to work very well, though. I tried catching the ball flipping the ball up out of my glove, dropping the glove off my hand and catching the ball in mid air. This seemed to work pretty well except that I often dropped the ball in the midst of the process or my glove stuck to my hand and I couldn't grab the ball in time. I continued to practice the process in bed each night. It finally became very natural and very fast. Through hours of practice, I could get the ball out of the glove and thrown back to Dad faster with one hand than he could get the ball back to me with two hands.

My leg was healing and finally got to the point where it could get a cast. In the spring of 1976, Dad put up two posts and tied a mattress up between them. He made a home plate from plywood and this became my backstop. We bought 12 baseballs and put them in an ice cream bucket. I picked up a ball, wound up, and threw over the plate and into the mattress. I picked up another ball and threw until the bucket was empty. I would go pick up all the balls and throw them again. Hour after hour I threw and threw, and then threw some more. Always trying to get more accurate and throwing harder each day. I was usually by myself and the hours were grueling.

Before the accident, I had been a great athlete, always picked first by the team captain on the playground. I was proud of that. I was a great athlete and everyone wanted me on their team. Then, after the accident when I got out on the playground, I had a cast on my leg and was missing an arm, and I was picked last. That was something that made me fight that much harder because I wanted to be the first one picked again. There are a lot of kids out there who never did have the chance to be picked first. Some have always been picked last.

The feelings of inferiority, not fitting in and just plain feeling like a loser set in. These feelings and thoughts that we have on the playground seem to creep into our schooling, our home life and eventually we start believing that we're not worth anything. Sometimes those kids turn away from life, and end up in trouble as they choose paths that lead them away from the good things in life. But through the months and years, I kept improving. In fifth grade, I got the cast off. I still had to hop to get around, but it seemed like each month I moved up one spot when we picked teams. I was the second to the last player picked, then I was picked in the middle. After a while, I was one of the first kids picked again.

My dream as a youngster with two arms of being a great football player turned into a dream of a one-armed youngster becoming a great basketball or baseball player. The dream of winning did not change, just the field that the winning was accomplished on.

My spirit was strong, my faith was strong and my determination was endless.

**From the Omaha World-Herald**

Plucky Lyons boy toughs it out
(March 9, 1977)

A year and a half-ago Ronnie Gustafson used to write stories in Jerry Mathers' fourth grade class about how someday he would be a professional baseball and football star.

It was fanciful stuff born of boyish dreams.

But there was a foundation of truth, too. At 9, Ronnie Gustafson already had impressed schoolmates and teachers with his athletic ability.

He came by his talents naturally—for his is an athletic family. His father, Don, 265 pounds and 6 feet 6 inches tall, is a former athlete who as a town team basketball player once scored 65 points in a game.

Ronnie has three older brothers, all athletes. Rick, 20, played baseball at Nebraska's Midland Lutheran College, Mike, 19, started at tight end for

Augustana College of Sioux Falls, S.D., last fall. Jim, 16, a sophomore at Lyons High School, played varsity basketball this winter. He might have been the school's no. 1 quarterback last fall had he not broken his wrist.

And then there is Ronnie. Some friends and sports and the family farm northeast of Lyons. It was there he worked and played with athletically gifted brothers and dreamed those dreams of future glory.

Jerry Mathers did. "At 7, he was competing with boys two and three years older," he said. "I coach a kid baseball team but Ronnie could throw so hard, I was afraid to have him cut loose. I was afraid for the batters."

Ronnie threw right-handed. And he played with an enthusiasm and intensity that comes from a competitor's heart. Evelyn Petersen, elementary head teacher at Lyons, remembers that as a second grader he was "a good student and a tremendous athlete. His coordination was much more refined than most children that age."

Ronnie has the size to accompany

his skills. Even as a fourth grader he showed indications that—like his father—he would be a big man.

He had started fourth grade in late summer of 1975. Then—as now—his world had revolved around school, thought he would be the best of them all.

And then the afternoon of Tuesday, Sept. 9 arrived. Ronnie, home from school, was helping his father with chores. They had hitched a wagon to a tractor. As he had done so many times before, Ronnie had hopped on the right fender beside his dad. They had started out when the unforeseen—the seemingly impossible—occurred.

A mechanism designed to keep the giant wheel rotating in conjunction

*continued on next page*

with the huge metal disc to which it was attached apparently slipped. Thrust ahead by its own weight and momentum, the wheel began revolving around the disc, shearing away bolts and twisting itself free as a bottle cap twists from its container.

Then it was loose, rolling on a mindless course of its own. In that instant the tractor lurched sideways, hurling Ronnie to the ground. Now, where the rubber wheel had been, there was only the circular metal rim—hard and sharp And in one awful moment, it past over the prostrate boy, severing him forever from his strong right arm and shoulder. As the frantic father fought for control, the rim also gouged and crushed the boy's right leg.

Today, Ronnie does not recall the sickening instant of impact. He remembers the wheel veering from the tractor, remembers falling. His next memory is that of his anguished father picking him up, pressing the gaping wound against his own body, and running the quarter of a mile back to his house. He remembers the trip in the Lyons Rescue Squad ambulance to Fremont's Dodge County Memorial Hospital 37 miles away.

He was conscious through the ordeal. So he remembers. So does Jon Heideman, the 27-year-old insurance agent and a member of the Lyons Volunteer Fire Department, which operates the rescue squad.

Heideman was among those answering the call to the Gustafson home. Now, 17 months later, he remains amazed at Ronnie's reactions. "He was so calm, so brave he just sparked everybody," Heideman said. He remembers the boy even sought to encourage his distraught parents: "Mom, mom, don't cry. I'll be all right."

It was six weeks before Ronnie came home—a hard six weeks.

There was pain and skin grafts and operations as doctors labored to restore the battered right leg for us.

And Ronnie? "I just knew I had to tough it out," he said. "I prayed for strength."

While he fought, a community responded to help one of its own. A Ronnie Gustafson Fund was begun at the First National Bank of Lyons. So far, a bank official said, $5,500 has been donated.

There were prayers. They were said at the Lyons United Methodist Church the Gustafsons attend and they were said in other churches and homes.

Prayers were answered. Ronnie lived. And one day he returned to school and Jerry Mathers' fourth grade class. He came back, Mathers remembers, with a grin on his face and the same competitive fire in his heart.

*continued on next page*

"Ronnie had left as a leader and nothing had changed," Mathers said. "He was still a leader. The kids looked up to him as one who knew how to act in a time of crisis."

They still do.

When you are 10 or 12, it is difficult to put feelings into words. It is hard to define inspiration. But Jeff Schoch, a 10-year-old classmate, tried: "All the kids admire Ronnie. Watching him makes us want to be better persons, too."

Charley Jessen is 12, a sixth grader. "I guess he taught us how to handle something bad," he said. "Ever since what happened to him, I try to do better with what I have."

Said Mathers, "Ronnie is no different now than before. This is what I think is so unusual."

The teacher remembers that when Ronnie returned, his leg would not permit him to participate in physical education.

"When the rest of the class went to the gym, we'd play our own game of basketball," Mathers said. "We would go around the room shooting at the wastebasket with a little ball. Know what? I couldn't beat him."

Said Miss Petersen: "I had Ronnie in second grade. He was a very open little guy—and still is."

Ronnie still wears a cast. There is a gap in the major bone below his knee where the tractor left its mark. He experiences bouts with osteomyelitis, an inflammatory disease of the bone. Doctors, however, are hoping of starting bone graft procedures this summer

But even with a cast, Ronnie was back competing this winter. Mathers was among teachers who conducted a Saturday basketball program for Lyons youngsters. He coached the grade school boys who reported.

Among them was Ronnie Gustafson.

"He asked no favors," Mathers said. "He played with no concessions and even with the cast he went stomping up and down the court as fast as he could go."

But shooting was difficult. At first his efforts were feeble and faltering. But Ronnie never gave up. "By the end of the season, he was making shots—some from as far out as the free throw circle," Mathers said. "His spirit is indomitable."

During the season, Ronnie played in grade school basketball games conducted between halves of the varsity high school contests. Among those who saw him was the principal of a rival high school. He sent Ronnie a letter. "I would like to tell you what a brave young man I thought you were," he wrote. "A young girl at our school who was in an auto wreck, saw you play. By your example, she, too, has decided to play again."

*continued on next page*

Ron has hopes of playing more basketball. Last summer, his father bought him 12 new baseballs. Each day, Ronnie would throw them over a homemade plate and into a mattress backstop. He would work for hours, retrieving the balls and then throwing them again and again, as he labored on his new "southpaw" delivery.

This fall he tried something new—baritone horn. Success there, however, has not been instantaneous. Said his mother: "When his brothers were home on Christmas vacation, they hid the mouthpiece so he couldn't practice."

Last week, she said, her son came home with a first-place ribbon won at a Lyons art show. That was a surprise. But Ronnie is full of them. A week after he first returned from the hospital, he was tying his own shoelaces. No one taught him—he did it on his own.

"We haven't babied him," his father said. "We have put our faith in the doctor and in God."

Has either parent been surprised at how well Ronnie has responded to adversity?

"No," Mrs. Gustafson said. "This is Ron's ways. We expected him to adjust."

And the future?

"We will let the Lord take care of that," she said.

And Ron?

Dreams die slowly in a fighter's heart.

"If they can just fix my leg," he said, "I may play pro football yet."

**From the Fremont Tribune**
A remarkable young man
(August 9, 1977)

Pee-wee no-hitters are a dime a dozen, 15 cents at the most.

Nothing unusual about a no-hitter in pee-wees. Certainly nothing worth mentioning in a column, right?

Well, that's where you're wrong.

A young Lyons athlete, Ronnie Gustafson deserves special citation here.

Gustafson pitched two no-hitters this season—two solid gold no-hitters.

What makes his feat so noteworthy is that he has only one arm, the left. And until losing his right arm in a terrible farm accident September 9, 1975, he was a right-hander.

"Ronnie Gustafson has more courage than anybody I've ever known, and that includes adults. He's absolutely one of a kind. He's remarkable. He is...well, golly, there just are

no words to describe the kind of kid he is," said Jerry Mathers of Lyons, Ronnie's fourth-grade teacher and one who has taken special interest in and time with the youngest son of Don Gustafson, of rural Lyons.

Greatest righty ever seen.

Ronnie Gustafson was destined to be an athlete. His father, a giant of a man at 6-6 and 265-pounds, was a great one, as are his older brothers, Rick, Mike and Jim.

Only there was something extra special about Ronnie.

"I really feel he would have been the greatest and biggest of all of us. None of the rest of us possessed the kind of physical potential at age 11 that Ronnie has. He could be bigger than dad," said Rick, the oldest of the athletic Gustafson brothers.

"All of the Gustafsons were far above most of the rest of their classmates as far as athletic talent was concerned. But Ronnie was further

ahead, comparatively, than any of the others," said Mathers, who was Ronnie's instructor the year the rim of the tractor wheel crushed his right arm, forcing amputation near the neck.

Showing outstanding ability in all sports, he appeared particularly talented in baseball.

"He was, without the slightest doubt, the greatest young right-handed thrower I've ever seen," said Mathers.

A phenom.

In order to fully understand the depth of young Mr. Gustafson's 360-degree turn, you have to appreciate his incredible ability as a right-handed pee-wee.

He was a phenom.

"Ever since he was 7 he played with the 11-12 age group in Lyons because he was too big, too good and threw too fast for his own age group," brother Rick said.

*continued on next page*

As an 8-year-old he once struck out nine 11-12 year-olds in a three inning span. He's batted over .600 in pee-wees (the 11-12 group) for five years running. He batted 1.000 at age 7 in the 7-8 age group.

Then came the horrible accident where he lost his right arm and severely injured his right leg. (The leg has had nine operations, it pains him terribly at times and, "it's still not out of danger yet," Mathers said.)

The phenom was suddenly without his strong, talented right arm, and almost without his right leg.

"He never once moped about it or felt sorry for himself. He went right to work on making the most of the one-arm and the one good leg he had left. On his very first day home from the hospital he was tying his shoelaces all by himself left-handed. And after he got his shoelaces on he went out and shot baskets," Rick Gustafson said.

The idea of switching positions after he lost his right arm never entered his mind.

"That's all he ever wanted to be, and the accident didn't change his mind. My brothers and dad and I set up a mattress, some posts, a plate, a pitching rubber and a bucket of balls, and he went right to work. He was determined to be as good left-handed as he ever was right-handed. It was a sight to behold his perseverance, determination, guts, desire... We just loved him for it," said the oldest Gustafson brother, a pitcher for the Oakland town team.

Ronnie's dedication resulted in a 6-1 record, including two no-hitters, and a .600 batting average. One no-hitter came in the league tournament. Lyons won the tourney as the littlest Gustafson pitched two complete games in a 48-hour span.

"He only struck out twice all season," Rick proudly said.

That's remarkable considering he had only one hand - his left, to boot - to hold the bat.

But everything about 11-year-old Ronnie Gustafson is remarkable.

No frustrating moments.

Incredibly, the transition from right hander with two arms to left hander with one arm presented no problems whatsoever.

"He's never had any frustrating moments. He's always been pretty ambidextrous. It wasn't nearly as great a transition for him as it would have been for most other kids," said Rick.

Because the sixth-grader-to-be hasn't as much as a shoulder on his right side, the possibility of developing an artificial limb to help him out seem remote.

What's that do to his future as a Lyons Lion?

"Wouldn't you say that at least 50
continued on next page

> percent of an athlete's success is desire? Ronnie has more desire than any person, child or adult, I've known. He plays basketball as well as he does baseball, and he's already talking about being a center or tight end in football. I don't think there's any doubt he'll be a star in every sport," Mathers said.
>
> Keep your eyes on this kid.

Even though some of the tools that I was utilizing to become a great athlete had been torn from my body, the heart, the grit, the desire and the determination from within me were still intact.

The people in Lyons were so supportive of me and my desire to live. But they were of the attitude that I had lost my opportunity to be an athlete like the rest of my family. My burning desire for success in athletics had not been destroyed.

I was driven to become the athlete I always wanted to be—to continue to dream and chase the dream that was before me. To become all that God wanted me to be. I was out to prove the doubters wrong. But there was a price to pay.

# 8

## The Long Road Ahead

The healing of my body continued, my growth continued and my desire to succeed continued. I started on the seventh-grade basketball team. Jerry Mathers, my fourth-grade teacher, once again was in my life as my junior high basketball coach. He was my biggest fan. I still had a brace on my leg and didn't run very well.

Coach Mathers devised a scheme where I always played offense. In essence I played half court. The rest of my team played a tenacious 2-2 zone or a box zone on defense. When they got the rebound they would use a baseball pass to move the ball down to me quickly. I quickly caught the ball and shot for the score. After six or eight quick points, our opposition had to respond by sending one of their men back to play defense on me the whole game.

**Following are the thoughts and recollections of Jerry Mathers:**

"On his ninth birthday, Ronnie Gustafson thought the world was his oyster. And why not? He was the biggest kid in his fourth-grade class at school by far. He was the best in every sport. Everyone thought he was going to be the biggest and best of all the four Gustafson brothers in athletics.

"Everyone's worst nightmare happened to Ronnie on

Sept. 9, 1975. I heard about the accident and rushed to the hospital in Fremont. Don, his dad, was blaming himself for what happened. His family rallied behind him and despite all predictions of death, and later predictions of a long hospital stay, Ronnie was home after just six weeks in the hospital. He was ready to come back to school on a part-time basis after eight weeks.

"Don brought an old overstuffed chair into the classroom with a footstool for Ronnie to prop his leg on. Every morning Don drove up to the front doors of the school and carried Ronnie up the stairs and planted him in that chair. Ronnie had an infection in his leg and a huge open wound. The smell of the infection could have affected weak fourth-graders but they were magnificent. They did not stare, nor ignore the wounds. They treated Ronnie as if he were just a regular student again. They were a lively group, but not once all year did I have a smidgen of a discipline problem.

"At noon hour, I stayed in the classroom with Ronnie. The others vied for the privilege of bringing up our lunches from the downstairs lunchroom. Ronnie was up hobbling around the room. He brought a tennis ball one day. 'I've got to learn to pitch left-handed,' he said. We threw diagonally across the room to each other. Ronnie soon had his control over throwing. He was soon throwing the ball hard. He was soon knocking holes in the walls. He was way too fast for a small classroom. We soon had to switch to basketball. We shot the tennis ball into a trash can. We played H-O-R-S-E. At first Ronnie had trouble shooting left handed. Quite a basketball shooter myself, I thought I would let Ronnie win a few games just to buoy up his spirits. Well, that idea lasted for about two days. Ronnie improved rapidly. Now I was shooting my best. Ronnie kept score of each day's games and the overall total on the chalkboard. Soon it was a fifty-fifty deal. He started hitting circus shots from all over the room. I can still see him hobbling up to the board to chalk up another victory for him, and of course, another loss for me. Meanwhile, chuckling that evil little snicker of his!

"By the seventh grade, Ronnie had recovered a great deal and continued to grow. His leg still created problems running. How was he going to play on my seventh-grade basketball team? We were a full-court pressing team that would fast break and were always putting pressure on the ball. Ronnie and I talked it over—you could discuss anything with him just as an adult, he was so intelligent. We agreed on this strategy: Ronnie just played half court, on the offensive end. His teammates played a 2-2 zone on defense. When they got the rebound, they turned and threw the ball down court to Ronnie. As soon as the other team saw him score three or four baskets in a row, they were quickly forced to take a person out of their offense to defend him. It worked! In effect, his offense turned into our best defense.

"Sometimes Ronnie intercepted the ball as the opponent made the inbound pass. We pressed the opposition and he stole the ball regularly and turned to the basket and scored. Other times he rifled these bullet passes to a teammate coming across the lane. He averaged 11 points a game in seventh grade.

"I planned to use Ronnie the same way his eighth-grade year. No! He insisted on running the court and playing defense. He became our top rebounder by going straight up off his good leg and snatching the ball with one hand out of midair.

"He insisted we play a man-to man defense and he worked so hard. He played through incredible pain each night. He never asked for any favors. He just competed. He never knew the word 'handicapped.' It simply wasn't part of his vocabulary. And more importantly it was not part of his life. I always hounded him about working on his right hand-ed dribbling. He just looked at me each time and whipped the ball behind his back, and said 'This is all I need!' His behind the back dribble going to his right really was awesome.

"Other teams knew they had to give Ronnie full attention on defense. He just about killed himself getting up and down the court to play. He was, and still is, an inspiration to his teammates, coaches and opponents.

"I have never met a braver person of any age than Ronnie. I know wounded war veterans, survivors of terrible accidents, survivors of massive heart attacks and other horrendous trauma. But few met their pain and problems so 'head-on,' so optimistically as Ronnie did. Not once did I ever hear him complain either of the pain, or of his many and varied problems, or of many skin and bone grafts and other major surgeries that continued for years. Not once did he rue his future, or ponder on 'What might have been...'"

By my eighth-grade year, I was out of the brace and running and jumping primarily using my "good" leg. My strength and endurance continued to grow along with my passion for basketball.

I played full court my eighth-grade season and competed with the rest of the kids. I was very average but continued to work hard.

Greg Kamp, the high school basketball coach who had coached all my older brothers, sat on the stage of the gymnasium and watched our junior high games. He apparently did not think I had the skills to compete at the high school level and told some people that "the one-armed Gustafson kid" can play junior high basketball, but he will never be able to compete at the high school level.

I heard about that comment and his words were drilled into my memory as if they were chiseled in granite. He knew how athletic the Gustafson family was. Why did he say this? This statement motivated me to a new level. I was determined to never, ever show pain or frustration and I was determined to never let him see me fail. I was mad. This anger was funneled into an endless geyser of determination.

I worked very hard on the farm. I threw hay bales, scooped corn and worked on equipment always focusing on doing the best I could do and becoming stronger; always focusing on the next goal of playing high school basketball. I spent many hours shooting and working on my ball-handling skills.

My family never took it easy on me. They always expected me to do the same work on the farm that they did. Having one arm was never an excuse for not being able to do something. It was expected that I could figure out any challenge that came my way.

Those challenges seemed to come on a regular basis. On the farm, we learned how to drive when we were 11 or 12. How does a one-armed guy learn how to drive a truck which has a clutch and a stick shift? Well, it can be done. I used my right knee to hold the steering wheel, my left foot on the clutch, as I reached across to the stick shift to shift. It was quite a chore.

Hooking up the hydraulic hoses on a farm implement was also a great challenge. Holding a bolt and tightening up the nut, throwing bales, climbing a ladder, fixing fences, and getting a nail started in a board were all fun, frustrating and tearful activities.

We had grain storage bins on the farm. There is a ladder that is mounted to the side of the bin and runs straight up the side of it. The ladder is used to crawl up on top of the bin and crawling in one of the manholes on the top. I used to be scared to death to crawl up these ladders. I crawled up the ladder and released my hand from each rung as I progressed up the side and grabbed the next rung. It wasn't so bad until I reached the top where I was 30 to 40 feet in the air and released my hand on the top rung and attempted to grab the handle on the manhole door on the top of the bin. I always prayed that it wasn't wet or greasy. If it was, I was going to fall to the ground and flatten anything in my line of flight. Once I overcame the fear of going up the ladder, I had to face crawling down the ladder. Again coming off the top, there is a lip that extends approximately six inches over the edge. As I held on to something on the roof, I had to release and grab the top rung that was a blind grab under the lip. Each time I did it I was scared but didn't want to let dad know that I was scared to death.

Sometimes my drive and ambition to overcome the obstacles in my life were to my detriment. There were so many people around me who were ready and willing to help me out. I always wanted to prove to people that I could do anything someone with two arms could do. I worked for hours trying to accomplish a task, too embarrassed to ask for help or assistance. Many times it seemed like a long lonely road to overcoming obstacles. I just never wanted to let my family see me fail. I couldn't let them down. They had given up so much for me. I wanted to somehow repay them with being successful.

There were many days alone in the field when equipment broke down. I was a mile away from the house, had equipment worth over a hundred thousand dollars and had a broken component. I had to figure out how the equipment really worked and fix it by myself on the spot. These were invaluable lessons in my life. I had to think through a process and use whatever resources were available to get the job done.

That's exactly what I needed to do with athletics. I knew I was broken down, all by myself and needed to use the resources I had left to win the battle.

I came into my freshman year full of fire and desire. The words of Coach Kamp vividly etched in my mind, "He will never play for me at the high school level." I was out to see him eat his words.

The first day of tryouts for basketball, I came running out

of the locker room with a big ol' smile on my face. Coach Kamp just looked at me and shook his head. I was the last guy in the world who he wanted to see on the basketball court that night.

I was the slowest player on the team. I had the worst vertical leap on the team. I was one of the worst ball handlers on the team. I had the least endurance of anyone on the team. But I made the team.

After every practice, I stayed late and ran extra sets of lines to increase my speed and endurance. After running, I shot free throws even though I was physically exhausted. I was always the last player to leave the court and always left the court after a made basket. There was something about leaving on a made basket that brought closure to the practice.

I went home after the practices in pain and total exhaustion. I gave everything I had every time I stepped out onto the court. Mom and dad saw the pain and exhaustion first hand each night. But I never let coach Kamp see me hurting. I refused to let him have the pleasure of seeing me fail.

The physical make up of my body made it very difficult to run and play ball. My right leg, the damaged leg, was nearly two inches longer than my left leg. This created backaches and soreness on a constant basis. I have no feeling to touch, only pressure, from my knee down to my foot. The total range of motion in my right ankle was approximately one inch. My right foot does not rotate from side to side. I could not jump or explode off my right leg. My right knee was weak and irreparable.

I arrived home after practice and lay down on the floor in the living room with ice packs on my right ankle and knee. The swelling throbbed terribly and I simply thought about giving up. The words of my coach kept coming back to me, "He will never play for me at the high school level."

This continued to motivate me to get up and go to school and practice the next day.

Each practice got more and more painful throughout the season. Each game got more and more embarrassing for me.

I was the scrub of all scrubs on the junior varsity team. I assumed my position at the end of the bench during games. I worked harder eating popcorn at the end of the bench than I did the last three or four seconds that I got into the game.

I took a shower after the games and went home. I was a failure. I walked into the house and could not look my parents in the eye. I wondered what they were thinking of me. I just knew they were thinking that I was an embarrassment to our family. My brothers were all all-stars and here I was the scrub of all scrubs. The last guy on the bench. How could my parents lift their heads high when I was such a scrub? Why would they come to my games and embarrass themselves. I must not be working hard enough. I'd never be good at anything I did.

I went downstairs to my bedroom after those games and lay in my bed and began to cry. My pillow was soon soaked. I was mad, I was sad, I was frustrated. Most of all I was embarrassed. There had never been a Gustafson who had ever sat the bench. Then there was me—the one-armed Gustafson boy who would never amount to anything. I was becoming everything everyone else thought I was going to be, not what I knew I wanted to be.

One night after one of the games, my dad came downstairs to my bedroom. He knew I was crying and he sat on the side of my bed and told me a story.

### The Garbage Truck

"Ron, it doesn't matter who you are, what you are or where you are at in life, but a big garbage truck is going to back up right beside you. It's going to hoist up its load and it's going to dump its load of garbage right on top of you. At that very moment, you have a decision to make. You can either sit in that garbage, act like that garbage, smell like that garbage and be just like that garbage. Or you can process the garbage and turn out fertilizer and make everything around you turn green, grow and prosper." Dad walked across my bedroom floor and was on his way out of the room. As he passed through the door way, he stopped, turned around and pointed that huge index finger at me and said, "Son, it's up to you. What are you going to do about it?"

My dad was a man of few words, but I had better listen to the few words he gave me to think about. I took this story to heart and turned my focus back to my dreams and away from the pain and embarrassment of the moment. I was more determined than ever to chase my dream.

I knew my stamina, my speed and ball handling had to get better to get to the proverbial "next level." One of the daily drills I used over the next year was something my brother Jim had done. He dribbled a basketball around the four-mile section that our farm sat on. Three miles were on gravel and one mile on asphalt. I figured if I could run around the section to increase my endurance and dribble a basketball at the same time, I could kill two birds with one stone.

I started down the gravel road dribbling the ball and it inevitably hit a stone and bounced into the ditch. I followed the ball to the ditch to retrieve it and got back on the road. This happened hundreds of times over the course of the following months and years.

I remember a hot sunny August day when I was in the last mile of my four-mile run/dribble. I was hot, sweaty and tired. The end was in sight and a car came toward me, kicking up all sorts of dust on the dry country road. The car flew by and the dust flew into my eyes and caked on my sweaty body. I was all by myself, frustrated, tired and covered with mud. No one was there to encourage me or to cheer me on. It was up to me to keep going. The motivation had to come from within.

I remembered a statement my dad made to me in junior high. He told me I had to work twice as hard, be twice as good and be willing to pay the price to get a fair shake at anything I did. Whether it was basketball, music, or scholastics; I had to work twice as hard. He told me, "Life is not fair–it is not designed to be fair." Dad always left the conversation with, "Are you willing to pay the price?"

Running was a painful process. My body seemed to hurt all the time. My body was not designed to run or to exercise. My body was better suited for laying flat on a couch with a remote control in my hand. But I knew what I wanted, and yes, I was willing to pay the price, over and over again.

My brother, Jim, was playing basketball at the University of North Dakota at this time. During the summer after my freshman year, I went to the University of North Dakota basketball camp.

I got to the gym early for the opening night of camp. I began to shoot and get stretched out. The players were showing up and as usual, the one-on-one games began as each of the players was sizing up the competition. I challenged a player who looked to be a great challenge. He accepted my challenge after a long hesitation. It was obvious from the start that he was not trying his hardest. I drove to the basket and he literally let me go all the way to the hoop and score.

This really made my blood bubble. I had to somehow send a message to let him know that I was there to compete, not to let him take it easy on me.

A little embarrassment is sometimes good for competitive people. I decided to bounce the ball between his legs as I drove to the hoop. He did not like that at all. Many of the players were gathering around the court where we were playing as people realized what was going on. The crowd grew and I got more competitive as he got more competitive. The game went on for another 5 minutes and the whole camp was watching us play. The whistle sounded and the game ended and the camp began. Kevin, my friendly competitor, and I turned out to be great friends and hung out all week together.

Later in the week, the one-on-one tournament for the camp began and I had never competed in a tournament. I played the first game and won easily. I continued through the tournament and arrived in the finals that last day of camp. The fun part of this story is that I was to play Kevin in the finals–the same guy I had picked for the challenge the opening night of camp.

I had built a great friendship with him along with many other players. The court for the championship game was packed around the edges. The local news station had picked up on the "one-armed guy" at the University of North Dakota basketball camp and they were there with lights and camera.

Kevin and I started the game, friends off the court, fierce competitors on the court. We both knew we were playing for pride and the essence of competition.

I won the coin toss. We were to play to 15 points and the winner had to win by two points. I started with the ball and made my first few shots. I ran my score up to 12 in a hurry. The problem was Kevin hit his first shots and was also at 12.

We were both tired. The game was emotional and the audience was cheering for each point. The pressure was mounting and Kevin and I both went into a slump and missed four shots apiece. Each of us made turnaround jump shots. The score was tied at 14-14 and Kevin had the ball. He shot and the ball hit the rim and was headed out of bounds. We both went for the ball and ended up diving for it and trying to bounce it off each other as we went out of bounds. We landed in a heap and the referee awarded the ball to me.

I needed one basket to win the tournament. Since the accident, my hand had grown and my forearm was very strong. With this combination, I learned to palm the ball as a sixth-grader. My patented game-winning move incorporated a fake where I acted like I was shooting but then palmed the ball and it stuck to my hand. Kevin went hook, line and sinker after my fake, and even left his feet to block the apparent forthcoming shot attempt. I pulled the ball back down, drove to the left and went up with the lay-up for the game-winning shot.

The crowd stood to its feet and clapped, Kevin and I both had tears in our eyes as we had both given it all we had. We hugged each other and a special friendship–developed under the auspices of competition–was born.

I gained confidence in myself and in the game of basketball at that camp. I went to another state where no one knew me and competed with some great ball players. I made a statement with my game and knew I could compete anywhere I went.

Competitors and coaches always said they should defend me on the left side since this was the only way I could drive to the basket. The problem with this was my brothers had tried this method many years prior on the driveway and I developed all of my favorite moves to the right. My favorite was to take one dribble to the left, then dribble the ball behind my back and go off my left leg with a fade away shot. My brothers couldn't even block that one. Needless to say, having people play me to my left was a dream come true.

My sophomore season started. I was bigger, stronger and in better shape. I made the varsity basketball team and started on the team for the same coach who said I would never play for him at the high school level. I was really getting tired of the battle to train as hard as I was. The words of my father kept coming back to me every day, "You have to work twice as hard and be twice as good as everyone else to get a fair shot at it!" I lived on these words, but there were times when my body hurt, my mind was tired of the war going on inside of me and I thought it might be nice to live an average life, not having to work quite so hard or feel quite so much pain. This small victory, of starting on the varsity basketball team, in my life gave me a thirst for more. I wanted to be the best, to see how far I could go!

**Following are the thoughts and recollections of Greg Kamp, Lyons High School basketball coach:**

"I had some real concerns as the head coach of the high school basketball team as I watched Ron play junior high ball. There was no way he was going to make it at the high school level. Ron did not run the floor very well at all and I knew he needed to be able to do this to compete. His offensive skills were pretty good, but you had to wonder if he was going be able to control, shoot and take care of the basketball in high school where stronger, quicker players would be a larger challenge for him. I am sure I had thoughts that maybe someday he could play a limited role in a junior varsity game, but I really didn't know if he could put all the offensive and defensive skills together to play in a varsity game. Undoubtedly my biggest concerns were his ability to run up and down the floor for an extended period of time, or for long enough to be able to help a team.

"As his freshman year started, there was no doubt he was struggling with the rigors of practice and, as we feared, it was mostly the transition part of the game, not the skills.

He was really amazing with the basketball. He erased all of my fears about how he was going to handle the basketball. As he continued, you felt that maybe you might have to let him do what he could in the running and gradually work himself up to a point where he could do the workout that the rest of the team was doing. One thing I learned very quickly from 'Gus' is that he didn't want any special treatment. He never asked for any special workouts or attention and it was very clear he didn't feel sorry for himself. In fact Gus commanded respect both on and off the court, not because he had one arm but because of the fine young man he was and by the way he practiced so tremendously hard. He quickly turned into an excellent leader. He was always the last player to leave the court. Always trying to improve.

"I don't think any of his teammates or coaches really knew the pain he was in because he never used it as an excuse. There were times in practice where we were just reviewing our opponent and we had to slow Gus down, he was always diving for loose balls and his intensity never let up! Gus played the game of basketball the way it was intended. He played hard all of the time and he had fun doing it.

"Sometimes, as a coach when you wonder if it is all worth it, you just think back to the tremendous young men you coached and Gus is definitely one of those. He has a special place in my heart. He showed me what character and courage is all about."

It was special seeing Coach Kamp become a believer in Ron Gustafson. I had to earn his trust and belief in me as a player by showing up every night at practice and giving it my all. By being a leader on the team and encouraging the players around me. Coach Kamp became a great friend, mentor and teacher of the game.

I still went home hurting all over. My 6-foot-2 frame that carried 170 pounds felt like it was always on the verge of falling in a heap. I slept with ice packs on my knees, ankles and back. Every morning I got up slowly, gingerly stepped down on my right leg and limped upstairs to have breakfast. Dad's words kept coming back to me, "Are you willing to pay the price?" The answer was still, YES!

**From the Omaha World-Herald**

Building normal life in Lyons: Cager's one arm can reach far

(December 25, 1981)

Omaha, Nebraska—Sixteen years ago, on Christmas Eve, the caboose was hitched to the family of Don and Joyce Gustafson of Lyons, Neb.

Christmas has always overshadowed son Ronnie's birthday. As a result, his family has granted one of the few concessions ever made to Ronnie.

"A lot of times in the past, we've celebrated his birthday early—a month early or even six months early—so he wouldn't get cheated," the elder Gustafson said.

Ronnie doesn't like to be cheated. He grabs every opportunity to live a normal life—even though he has to do so with one hand.

A tractor accident when he was 9 cost Ronnie his right arm and nearly his right leg as well. But the youngest of four sons is doggedly following the athletic footsteps of his brothers.

Rick, the oldest, lives in Ames, Iowa, where he attends Iowa State and is a competitive weight-lifter. Mike recently graduated from Washington University in St. Louis with a degree in systems engineering. Jim, who played guard on Lyons' Class C (Nebraska) State Championship team in 1979, is a scholarship player at the University of North Dakota.

Ronnie, the only sophomore on the Lyons High School varsity, is a 6-foot-2 starter.

"I find myself thinking about it once in a while," said teammate Dave Anderson, a senior. "What would he be like if the accident hadn't happened? If he is this good with one arm, what would he be like with two?"

Some believe Ronnie would have been the best athlete of the Gustafson brothers.

*continued on next page*

"At 9," his father said, "I thought he had a little bit more talent than the others, but it was because his older brothers were always out there working with him."

Ronnie always wanted to be an athlete like his brothers. He tagged along with them wherever they went. Along the way, he picked up several nicknames.

"He got the nickname 'Charlie' even before the accident," the elder Gustafson said. "One of his older brothers' baseball coaches gave it to him. Ronnie would go along and sit on the bench. The coach got to liking him. They'd sit together and eat popcorn. Then, the coach started calling him Charlie."

"Pretty soon that was his name. When he graduated from a Sunday school class his teacher didn't even know his real name."

Ronnie was always ambitious. He had some hogs on the place east of the Gustafson farm that the elder Gustafson also farms. Ronnie's dad also had some cattle over there that required some tending. So they decided to ride there on the tractor and do their chores together.

There was the usual father-son banter, the kind that takes place between a man and his boy when they are doing things together. The tractor rumbled down the road.

Suddenly, it lurched to one side and Ronnie was thrown to the road. The rim on a rear wheel had worn and the tire slipped off.

"The cast-iron hub got him," his father said.

Ronnie's arm was severed at the shoulder. The tibia, the larger of the two bones in his right leg, was crushed. Circulation in his leg was so damaged that he eventually lost one toe and parts of two others.

Ronnie spent six weeks in the hospital. He has had 14 operations, the last about three years ago. After returning home, Ronnie quickly learned how to do things left-handed.

"I had a cast on my leg and I couldn't walk at all," Ronnie said. "It was a month before I could even go outside."

But Ronnie and his dad went to the garage. Ronnie sat on a chair and began to throw a baseball to his dad. They played catch hour after hour.

"It wasn't for the distance, it was for the accuracy," Ronnie said. "I was throwing at Dad's chest. It was for pure accuracy. I was pretty poor, but I always had people around to help out. Dad was always there.

"After a lot of hours, even after a couple of days, I could see the progress. After I could tell I was progressing, I always wanted to do more. When I'd get through throwing the baseball, I'd go outside and shoot some baskets."

continued on next page

The cast remained on his leg for more than a year, but that didn't hamper him when baseball season came. The Little League coaches in the area got together and made another of the few concessions. He could bat and a designated runner did the hoofing whenever contact with the ball was made.

That contact became more frequent over the years. It became obvious that Ronnie planned to continue his dream of following his athletic brothers.

"Even three or four years ago, when it looked like he wanted to play, I asked myself that question: 'What are we going to do when Ron gets to high school?' asked Greg Kamp, basketball coach at Lyons.

"Do we take it easy on him? Last year, when he was a freshman, that was my first instinct. But things changed after that first practice. I talked with him afterward and he said,

'Coach, I don't want to be treated any differently than anybody else.' He has made it easy for me. He doesn't ask for any favors and he doesn't expect any. He'll go out there and do what everyone else does."

Ronnie is blessed with a large hand. His left arm, because of constant use, is stronger than normal. He could palm a basketball in the sixth grade, not because his hand was large enough then, but because the strength in his forearm was so great that he could grip the ball tighter than others of his age.

Ronnie plays center, the hub of activity in basketball. His presence has required no adjustments on the part of his teammates.

"None at all," Anderson said. "The passes come just as hard to him as anyone else. There is respect for him. He is a lot more mature than most sophomores. I don't think people look at him as having one arm and being different."

Does the list of can-dos include changing directions by dribbling behind his back?

"That's what he does best," Kamp said.

"I do it all the time," Ronnie said. "I had to against my older brothers."

His brothers, according to their father, were instrumental in keeping the flame of competition alive.

"His brothers, whenever they were around, really poured it on him," the elder Gustafson said. "They really burned him up."

If there is a noticeable trace of the accident while Ronnie is on the court, it is that he runs with a limp. His right leg, the one he nearly lost, is nearly an inch and three-quarters longer than his left leg. Bone was taken from his hip and grafted into the crushed tibia.

"His ankle is stiff," Don Gustafson said. "I assume it's because he was in a cast for so long. The doctor said there is one more operation that would have a 50-50 chance of success. They would move some more muscle. It would take away the side movement to give more up-and-down movement in his ankle. But we figured he had been through enough. No more."

The elder Gustafson said the muscles in Ronnie's right leg have all been moved to the front or along the side of the shin area.

"All those operations were rough," the father said. "The skin grafting was especially painful. But he took it like a man, you might say."

**From the Oakland Independent**

Talk about inspiration
(February 4, 1982)

Anybody who thought the bottom line of the Oakland-Craig's boys basketball game with Lyons last Friday was whether we won or lost missed the whole point.

Over the years, I've seen some incredible moments of courage on the athletic field. I've seen kids play with a lot of heart. I've seen kids use the springboard of athletics to overcome some pretty big odds. I've seen guts, raw desire and talent maximized to the "nth" degree.

But, I have never in my life seen a more wonderful, more awe-inspiring moment in sports than when Lyons' Ron Gustafson took the basketball court against Oakland-Craig last Friday.

Anybody who didn't learn a little something about himself and about life by watching Ron Gustafson must be a robot.

Ron Gustafson is the greatest testimony to positive thinking I have ever encountered.

Most of you know the story. Ron lost his right arm and part of one leg in a farm accident several years ago. A ton of operations followed. Suddenly, the kid projected as the greatest of all the great Gustafson brothers was only "half a person."

Athletics? Surely this kid would have to forget about being an athlete. All those dreams of sports grandeur—the dreams that his three older brothers made into realities—would have to be chucked into file 13. It was inconceivable that a kid with such a severely limiting handicap could even think about becoming a high school athlete.

He's got a great mind and a great sense of humor. Surely he could accept the limitations of his handicap
continued on next page

and content himself with becoming super fan or a team statistician or a student manager.

I mean, good grief, the only arm he has left is his left—and he was right-handed! He can't run. He limps something awful. No, surely there was no way this kid could even think of continuing his quest for athletic stardom.

Don and Joyce Gustafson's youngest son decided that if life dealt you a lemon, you might as well make a lemon tree out of it—the best lemon tree ever grown, yielding the best lemon juice man has ever tasted.

Ron Gustafson is only a sophomore this year. He's not only a starter but also quite possibly the best basketball player on the Lyons team.

With an extraordinary amount of self-discipline, positive thinking, dedication, work! Work! Work! And, yes pain—the kind that you and I will never know in our lifetime—Ron made himself an athlete. Not merely an athlete. An outstanding athlete.

It's one thing to have a handicap and play baseball —which he does very well in the summer. He can play a position, first base, where he doesn't have to run quite so much. And there always are pinch-runners for him.

But basketball? No other sport requires quite so much of the arms and legs than basketball.

Young Mr. Gustafson dribbles behind his back. He can shoot with the best of them from 20 feet out. He can mix it up and rebound with the big boys. There are, perhaps, tougher defensive players than Ron—but not many. And I have never seen a high school kid rifle passes and assists the way he does. I can think of one who comes close; his all-class, all-state brother Jim, catalyst on that unbeaten Lyons team of '79, the best high school basketball player I have ever seen.

And Ron's only a sophomore. Heaven only knows how great this kid could become if he had two arms and two legs like the rest of us. But Ron doesn't dwell on what might have been. He dwells, instead, passionately, with what can be.

Ron Gustafson, ladies and gentlemen, is the living end. And thank goodness we'll get to watch him, and learn from him, another couple years yet.

I ended the season as a sophomore averaging six points, three rebounds and four assists per game.

My junior year was even better and I began to carry more and more leadership of the team, to motivate and keep the team heading down the right path. Each of the statistical categories got better. Seven points per game, six rebounds and five assists per game.

The excitement for my senior year was unbelievable. I dreamed of a marquee year. The season turned out to be filled with painful injuries and lackluster performance. I sprained my left ankle, the good one, and also had a deep thigh bruise in my left thigh. The injuries seemed to nag at me all season long.

The pressure to perform was also nagging at me. People were traveling from all around the area to come see this one-armed guy play. I heard about people coming to the game and felt that I really had to prove something. I never played as well as I wanted to. My mind was full of thoughts. If I had a bad game, the fans might say that I was a charity case. That I wasn't as good as the newspapers were saying. How did I stack up when college coaches came to see the games?

The numbers were better than my junior year, but not the numbers that I was shooting for. Ten points, eight rebounds and 7 assists per game.

I feared that my poor senior season would make it very difficult to earn a scholarship to the college level. Once again I had fallen short of my goal and had a decision to make. Should I give up or continue to chase my dream? Was there enough passion and desire left in me to continue the training regimen to take it to the next level?

# 9

## The College Experience

I had the opportunity to go to the University of Nebraska basketball camp in Lincoln the summer before my senior season. Once again I was in the one-on-one tournament and having a lot of fun winning as I worked my way through the brackets. My friends were very excited for me and kept watching my games and encouraging me.

The semifinals were set: Ron Gustafson versus Joel Hueser. My buddies were coming up to me and saying that I was good, but not that good. They asked if I knew who Joel Hueser was. I said "no." They let me know that he was one of the top scorers in the state and would most likely win the scoring title his senior year. Hueser was probably one of the top five players in the state, they said, and his dad was the head coach at Kearney State College. They didn't think I could beat him.

I told them I didn't care how good he was supposed to be, what he was supposed to do next season or that his dad was a head coach at the college level. All I knew was that Joel and I were going to be on the court, the game started out at zero to zero and that I was going to beat him. They walked away in disbelief.

The game started and I was shooting well. I was able to beat Joel and went on to the finals where I met a 6-foot-6-inch all-state performer from Wyoming.

Again, I was outmatched. He was bigger, stronger, faster, and boy could he jump. No one gave me a chance at winning this one. Talk about being outmatched.

The game was scheduled for after lunch with the whole camp watching. I skipped lunch and went back to the dorm room to listen to my Christopher Cross cassette of "Ride like the wind" several times. This song got me fired up. I felt I could conquer the world.

I left the dorm room and walked by myself to the coliseum. I was focused and determined to win. I was going to leave everything I had on the court. I knew he was a better athlete. I knew he had more skills and abilities than I had. But I also knew that I had more perseverance, guts, determination, heart and a burning desire to win that would take me the distance!

The game began, we exchanged baskets and he slowly pulled ahead by three points. We were playing to 15 and had to win by two points. I had the ball at the top of the key. I was tired, sweaty and down by three points. The score was 14 to 11. He only needed one basket to win.

Once again, the words from my dad popped into my mind. "Are you willing to pay the price?" I had been paying the price and I wasn't going to be stopped here. I wanted the win more than anything. I gritted my teeth. I was not going to be beaten.

I drove to my left, he stopped the drive so I dribbled behind my back, jumped off my left foot and shot a scoop shot. Dan fouled me and the ball went off the board and into the hoop. The basket was good and I shot the free throw to tie the game.

It was 14-14, meaning the next basket scored, won the game. Dan had the ball at the top of the key and drove to the basket. The ball hit the backboard, hit the front of the rim and bounced off. I got the rebound and dribbled to the top of the key. I knew I needed to score on this possession. If I didn't, I knew Dan was going to score on me and win the game. I was exhausted and knew I needed to finish strong and finish fast!

I checked the ball with Dan at the top of the key. I decided to try my game-winning move again. I palmed the ball, faked a shot from the top of the key and Dan jumped to try to block it. I pulled the ball back and drove to the basket for the game winner. The crowd went wild and Dan and I shook hands. There is magic in leaving all you have on the court. The magic of competition and having the heart to overcome the obstacles.

Because of this opportunity to play Joel Hueser in the semifinals, I now had the opportunity to visit Kearney State College. I had the chance to walk on there and chase my dream to play college ball. I went to Kearney and talked to Coach Jerry Hueser. He told me I had to prove myself to his coaching staff and that I should not expect any special treatment. I looked at him and told him all I wanted was a fair shot at playing basketball at Kearney State. I had never received any special treatment from my parents, my brothers or anyone else, and wasn't looking for anything special from him.

My move to Kearney was pretty scary. I didn't know anyone in Kearney and was not sure how this college life might affect me. This was all uncharted waters. I felt comfortable in Lyons and on the farm. I grew up there and knew all the ins and outs. Kearney was a whole new environment, new people, and so many unknowns. Basketball was at the center of my life, so as soon as I got moved into the dorm, I headed for Cushing Coliseum to get a workout in. The gym was beautiful and I was intimidated as I walked into the facility.

I was nervous, scared and kept asking myself, "Am I really good enough to play college basketball?" The doubts started creeping into my mind for the first time. What was I doing here? Why am I going to continue to put my body through the pain? Is it really worth it? Am I willing to pay the price?

As I shot around by myself, I relived some of the pain in my life. I dug deep into who I was and what I wanted to do; to play college basketball. This was my dream. Was I ready to chase after it?

A few guys showed up and we started a pick up game. Once I broke a sweat, the doubts left my mind and my competitive nature came out. This was a great lesson for me to learn. We all have doubts. We all have fears. The best thing to do when doubt and fear sets in, is to get up and go face it head on. Take action!

I simply had to go out on the court and do the things I had worked so hard to do and run the doubt out of my mind. I knew the crack of doubt could turn into the Grand Canyon of failure.

Tryouts began and I was playing great basketball. I felt that I was in a rhythm and things were going my way.

The last day of tryouts, the garbage truck that Dad told me about, backed up right beside me and dumped another load on me. I tore cartilage and tendons in my left knee. My season was over.

I had knee surgery and worked at getting back into shape. I knew I needed to process the garbage that was dumped on me and make something good happen. I needed to turn this setback into a comeback.

My sophomore year, tryouts were going well. During the final week though, I had more cartilage and tendon damage in my left knee. I had to have another knee surgery. My athletic career had come to an end.

I had pushed my body to peak performance over the last 18 years, and now my career had come to an end. It was time to hang up my basketball shoes.

I went back to my apartment that night and began to cry alone in my bedroom. How will I ever be able to tell my family that I was done, that I had failed to make it to the college level? I was a failure, a disgrace to the Gustafson family; the only Gustafson who did not play at the college level. I was a one-armed failure. What was left in life now? Life as I knew it had come to an end. Everyone who saw me would know that I was a failure; that I didn't make it. The media had given me so much attention and now I was done. I was going to be the laughingstock of the area.

The toughest phone call I have ever made was the night I called Mom and Dad to tell them that I was finished playing ball. I cried as I told them. I was at the lowest point of my life. I hit rock bottom. I had no where to turn. My world stopped spinning. I put so much pressure on myself to perform and achieve. I didn't want to be average. I felt that I had to prove to people all along my journey in life that I could be better at anything than anyone with two arms.

My parents always wanted me to give 110 percent, but they never put pressure on me. The pressure was self-imposed. There has always been something inside of me that pushes me.

I had poured my life into athletics. The game of basketball had been a daily habit for me. Six, seven, eight hours a day, seven days a week. Training, working, playing the game. And now it was over. What was I going to do? My life revolved around the game. I was left with nothing. No confidence, no dream, no zest for living and no direction. I couldn't understand how I could work so hard and never achieve my goal. I gave it my all. I persevered through the pain. I kept asking myself why I did it? Why did I work so hard? Why did I put myself through all the lonely hours in the driveway, in the gym and on the gravel roads? And now I had nothing to show for it.

Now that I was a sophomore at Kearney State College, I decided to start going to class. I even found the library. It was amazing!

Alcohol also became a big part of my life. My focus had always been athletics in high school. My desire to succeed in athletics outweighed any desire to drink, Dad made sure of that.

A couple of buddies and I went to a football game my junior year in high school. We picked up some peppermint schnapps on the way. This was my first experience with alcohol. I had a few drinks and was pretty tipsy. It didn't take much liquor to make me goofy. I got home and Mom and Dad knew I had been drinking. They didn't say anything to me that night. Dad woke me up at 5:30 the next morning and had me in a drying bin scooping corn.

It was hot and dusty in there. I felt like death warmed over. I scooped and scooped and felt as if my head was going to blow off due to the headache and I felt like throwing up.

I had the project done by 10 a.m. and crawled into the pickup with Dad to help feed the cattle. He looked at me and asked, "Was it worth it?" And that was all that was said. Needless to say, I did not drink again during high school.

Later, as a college student, no athletic career and wanting to be one of the guys, I started to drink and drink. And drink. My competitiveness is a strength, but it can also be a weakness. My desire was to out-drink anyone willing to sit down with me. And I did most nights.

My life took a downhill turn, in fact, I was on the bobsled of life, heading straight for hell at a high rate of speed. I was staying out late at night, stumbling home and in many cases didn't make it home. I was mistreating females and doing things that I knew were wrong. I was waking up in gutters, yards and alleys—and wondering how I got there.

The garbage truck had dumped on me. I was sitting in that garbage, acting like that garbage, smelling like that garbage and being just like that garbage.

My life had been very focused on athletics until that point and I finally realized that part of my life was over. Everything I did revolved around being prepared to compete. When basketball was over as a sophomore in college I had a lot of free time on my "hands." I started going to parties and meeting a lot of people. Naturally, when I went to a party, I typically ended up with a glass of beer in my hand. By nature, I'm an all-or-none type of guy. When I decide to do something, I do it to the best of my ability. Alcohol became another avenue to excel. The same desire and determination that helped me compete in athletics became an enemy as I began to drink.

When I worked out in the gym, I worked out until exhaustion. When I ran, I ran until I couldn't run any further. When I ate, I ate until the food was gone. And when I drank, I drank until the beer was gone. I had no concept of moderation in my life. I always gave everything I did 110 percent.

Athletics gave me notoriety, I met people, I was popular and it gave me so many "extras" that young people crave. When athletics were no longer there, partying and alcohol began to fill some of the void in my life. It allowed me to be popular, it gave me a false sense of knowing a lot of people and it gave me an escape from the pain of not playing ball.

The pain-killing drugs I received in the hospital gave me relief from the physical pain. I needed them to survive the pain every four hours. Basketball gave me an escape from my own reality. I could step on the court and dream about being Julius Erving or one of my brothers. I had control of the game once I set foot on the court. It was like my security blanket to some extent. Alcohol became my new pain killer. It took me away from what I saw as a failure in athletics. I didn't reach my goal to play college basketball and I felt like a failure. Alcohol seemed to numb the pain and helped me meet people so that some of my personal needs were being met. Popularity, notoriety, recognition and humor all seem to flow out of the parties I was going to. I really enjoyed all the attention.

Drinking started out to be a weekend habit on Friday or Saturday night. It evolved into Friday and Saturday night. The monster grew into three, four and five nights a week. I often woke up with a headache, felt rotten and eventually realized that drinking another beer for breakfast took the edge off the hangover. Again, not being able to stop at one beer drew me to two, three, four and so on. It was amazing how creative I was in hiding my bad habit. I used a convenience store cup with ice in it filled with beer and sipped on it in the mornings on my way to class. This might have been the first clue that something was way out of alignment in my life.

I still went over to the coliseum on the weekends to play in pick up games. One day, I found myself guarding a man who was very good, a fellow named Sid. This really got my blood pumping to compete again. We went nose to nose and played very hard. After the game we sat down to take off our shoes. He initiated a conversation with me. He asked me if I wanted to go to lunch with him.

Since I was a starving college student, I asked him if he were buying. When he agreed, I said, "Let's go!"

# 10

## Forsaking All I Trust Him

Sid and I built a wonderful relationship. We went to ball games together. He and his wife Karen had me over for dinner and we just hung out together. I liked Sid a lot. There was something that drew me to him.

He was athletic, a family man, competitive, outgoing and excited about life. The only thing he had going against him was that he was a youth pastor at a church and did not drink. At that time, I reasoned that five good qualities out of six was OK.

Sid invited me to one of his Sunday school classes to talk to the high school group about my life. I really enjoyed the opportunity to share my victories with the students. This was my first speaking engagement.

Sid and Karen invited me to stay for church that day, so I did. Pastor John McNeil preached a great sermon. He was passionate about his faith and his preaching really got my attention. When I met Pastor John after the service he looked me in the eye, shook my hand, and made me feel like I was the only one in the whole church. That really impressed me.

I continued going to church at this Evangelical Free Church.

Sid got me plugged into a Bible study. I was raised in a church-going family, but we never opened the Bible to see what it really had to say to us. I went to church while growing up, but just went through the motions. This concept of studying the Bible was intriguing. It was filled with stories of men failing and then turning to God for strength, wisdom and direction in their lives.

My typical weekend consisted of partying on Friday and Saturday and making it to church on Sunday morning slightly hung-over. My desire for alcohol and the partying seemed to diminish as I learned more about the Christian faith. I was memorizing scripture and learning that the Bible wasn't a book of don'ts, but a book of dos. It was an operator's manual for life.

Sid spoke at a retreat one weekend and his topic was faith. He talked about an acrostic for FAITH:

**F**orsaking
**A**ll
**I**
**T**rust
**H**im

This intrigued me. He expanded upon faith and the trust we can all have through a relationship with Jesus Christ. I had never heard someone talk about a relationship with Jesus. I always thought that if you believed in God, didn't break the rules, and were nice to people that you were a shoe-in to make it to heaven.

Sid taught from the scripture that evening that we all fall short of the mark and that we can never be good enough to earn a relationship with God. He challenged each of us to simply place our faith in Jesus Christ.

What is faith? Sid used a wonderful analogy that helped me to understand. Sid said a man went to Niagara Falls and strung a tightrope across the waterfall and attached each end to a rock. The wire ran over the waterfall and the rugged rocks that were under the water. The man stood up and asked if anyone believed that he could walk across Niagara Falls on a tightrope. People began to gather around him. They thought he was out of his mind and was trying to kill himself.

He walked across on the tightrope, turned around at the other side and walked back. By this time, thousands of people had gathered to watch this person they thought was a lunatic and wondered what he was going to do.

He then asked the crowd if anyone believed in him enough to think he could walk across Niagara Falls on a tightrope while pushing a wheelbarrow. The people thought he was going to kill himself.

He placed the wheelbarrow on the rope, pushed it across the rope, turned around and pushed it back. The crowd was going nuts. They were cheering and believing this guy could do anything. He could do it all. He was amazing!

He turned to the crowd and asked, "Do any of you believe in me enough to think that I can push a wheelbarrow with someone in it across Niagara Falls on a tightrope?" The entire crowd started to chant, yes, yes, yes, yes. He addressed the crowd and asked, "Which one of you wants to be the person in the wheelbarrow?" The crowd quieted down and there were no volunteers.

This is what Sid meant by faith; believing so much that you would put your life in the wheelbarrow and allow Jesus to carry you through this game of life. I had great "head" knowledge of who Jesus Christ was and what He did for me, but I hadn't allowed this knowledge to capture my heart and place my life in his wheelbarrow.

I had been active in religious activities, going to church, yet I was still wondering how I was going be judged. I had acknowledged some religious principles and tried to do the right things, but I had never placed 100 percent of my faith in a relationship with Jesus Christ. Sid told me that God loved me so much He sent his Son to pay the penalty for my sins. Jesus Christ died as a sacrifice in my place, submitting to death on a cross in order to give me life eternal. He was dead and buried, but He rose on the third day. We know this is true for He was seen by more than 500 people, and their lives were changed because of their newfound relationship with Christ. Sid said that if I confess with my mouth that Jesus is Lord and believe in my heart that God raised Him from the dead that I would be saved.

I went to my apartment that night and thought about what Sid said. On my knees next to my bed, I prayed to accept Jesus Christ as my Lord and savior. I took the next step and placed my total trust in Him and what He did for me on the cross. He had total ownership of my life. I was His.

I felt a huge load off my back. No longer did I have to perform at a certain level to gain respect or to prove a point. I found the freedom that can only be found in Christ. I was a changed man, a free man. No matter what was happening in my life, I was going to let God use me to do what ever he wanted me to do.

FAITH—Forsaking All I Trust Him!

What does a one-armed guy do in life when all I knew up to this point was basketball? My self worth and significance had all come from my performance on the court. Basketball gave me notoriety and recognition. My perceived personal value was equal to my last performance. When I had hit rock bottom God brought an incredible man into my life by the name of Sid Huston. He provided the answers to life's many questions and provided a great foundation in my faith in Jesus Christ. My newfound relationship with Christ truly changed my life and gave it meaning and direction. I suddenly had true value. I was valued so much that God's son, Jesus Christ, died for me.

I am so blessed to have met Sid. He is such a neat guy. He also played college ball. We got to know each other pretty well. He was a very competitive guy and had succeeded at many things. His competitive spirit reminded me of myself in a grownup's body. I liked Sid. He was great to be around. He had such wisdom, character and integrity in his life and in his family. He was the only guy in the world who could have captured my attention to spiritual life. He went nose to nose with me in sharing his faith with me.

**Following are the recollections and thoughts of Sid Huston, youth pastor:**

"As youth and college pastor and basketball devotee, I hung around the college gym at basketball tryout time. If you love intense basketball, tryouts are when you see the prospects lay it all out. This particular year I was amazed as a 'one-armed Wonder' was not only keeping up, but he was making the plays. This guy was grabbing the bounds, making the passes and hitting the shots. He was doing it minus an arm and an obvious limp.

"I was drawn to this young man named Gus. What I was drawn to was his spirit to overcome anything. The kind of spirit that just keeps climbing when you have been told the wall is insurmountable. I needed this attitude in my life. I went out of my way to meet Gus. We got into some pickup games. We entered into one of the most fruitful relationships of my life.

"As a youth pastor, I wanted so much for Gus's spirit to rub off on the youth I was working with. They were always so down and he was always so up. They didn't stay down for long after meeting Gus. Gus has a gift at uplifting the human spirit. It is not just his story, or his personality; it also has something to do with his faith. Be inspired!"

Sid had a profound impact on my life. All those Cokes we used to drink and the stories he used to teach me about the scriptures were incredible. The lessons of life have stuck with me as I raise and train my family today.

# 11

## The Woman of My Dreams

One of my parents' greatest fears for me was that of finding a wife and having a family. They were worried that a nice young lady may not be willing to marry a man with a handicap. They feared that I may never have the blessing of having a loving wife and children. Little did they know that God had the perfect woman picked out for me.

Julie Graham and I met at a doughnut shop in Kearney, Nebraska, at approximately 1 a.m. I was there studying during finals week my junior year with a friend of mine. This was a typical studying location for me. Where else could you have fresh doughnuts and a bottomless pot of coffee to assist with the grueling expectations of professors? It seemed that if I went to the library on campus I ended up socializing and not getting any studying done.

As Bobby Betzold and I were studying, two attractive, radiant girls came in to get some doughnuts and hot chocolate. Their birthdays were both during finals week. So they finished their tests and were out having fun celebrating. I have to admit, I needed a break from studying and talking to two beautiful young ladies was right up my alley.

The girls came over to our table and Bobby and I were trying to impress them with our studious nature. We visited and they seemed to be wonderful women. We talked about plans for Christmas vacation and other small talk. They said they were in a sorority and had to move into new rooms the next semester, so I took it upon myself to ask for their new phone numbers. They wrote "Jody" and "Julie" by their phone numbers and put a smiley face at the bottom of the napkin with the words CALL US AFTER CHRISTMAS! I have never been accused of being overly bright, but this one was obvious.

I did some background checking on the girls. I recalled from our brief conversation that Julie was from Grand Island, Nebraska. I had a great friend and fraternity brother, Doug Bonnesson, who was also from Grand Island. I wondered what the chances would be of Doug knowing her. So I called him to get the inside information and it turned out that he had gone to high school with her and they were close friends. I asked what she was like and he gave me a rave review. She was kind, caring and wonderful. He gave Julie two thumbs up!

After the Christmas break, I took the initiative to call Julie. I tried to be real cool and casually asked her to go out on the evening of January 14th. I only had one problem, I couldn't remember which one of the girls was Julie and which was Jody. My biggest fear was showing up at the door and having both of them there. Which one was I going to look at? If I picked the wrong one, I was toast.

Julie had her own issues to deal with after accepting a night out with this one-armed guy named Gus. I had a colorful past with girls. Julie's friends in the sorority knew she was sweet, innocent, caring and sensitive. When they learned she was going out with me they tried to convince her I wasn't her type. I had a bad reputation and they were trying to protect their friend. Thank God, Julie didn't listen to them.

The morning of our date, I was walking to class. Either Jody or Julie was walking toward me. I began to panic since I didn't know which girl she was. Was this Julie, my date tonight? We visited briefly and she said she was excited to go out tonight. What a relief. I finally knew which one she was. This took off most of the pressure.

I drove up to her house that night, walked up to the door and knocked. I recall just staring at Julie as she opened the door. She was glowingly beautiful. I remember freezing for a moment and feeling unusual at the time. I walked Julie to my car, a 1977 Buick Regal that was two-tone, green and mostly rust, and opened the door for her. She got in and my mind was racing.

Julie was the first girl I had dated since making a decision to trust Christ's direction in my life. I wasn't sure what to say or do because I wanted to respect and honor the girl I was dating and really change this aspect of my life. I had taken an Amy Grant (a popular contemporary Christian singer) cassette with me and had it in my tape deck. I got in the car and started the engine. I then pushed the cassette in and the music began to play. She was startled a bit and looked at me. She said, "This is my favorite cassette!" I knew we were off to a great start. I had a feeling at that very moment that I was going to marry this girl. I had never had a feeling like that before and it put an incredible amount of pressure on me.

We went to a very romantic basketball game, of course. We sat with a bunch of my buddies and we went out for nachos afterward. We sat and talked until the restaurant closed. We talked about each other's pasts, our families and of all things, what we would do if we won a million dollars. I had never talked about such personal things in my life with a girl. This was exciting and scary at the same time.

Julie and I continued to date. We spent countless hours sitting on the couch talking about life, our personal goals and the future. We were total opposites. My goals revolved around business success, building businesses and ruling the world, of course. Julie's goals were built on educating mentally handicapped students in the classroom, having a family and making cookies for the neighborhood kids. She was a special education major, which matched perfectly with her caring, loving, sensitive nature.

We dated for 18 months. I was a year older than Julie and graduated with a degree in marketing in May of 1988. After our third date we had openly talked about getting married. We knew it was a match made in heaven, at least for me. I had just accepted a sales position with a company in Omaha, was set to graduate and needed to solidify our future together. I was ready to propose and ask this incredible woman to spend the rest of our lives together.

On the evening of April 14th, I drove to Grand Island to ask Julie's father, Gary Graham, for permission to marry his daughter. I was nervous not knowing exactly how a father, any father, was going to feel having his daughter marry a one-armed guy. I'm sure not all fathers dream about their daughter's knight in shining armor having one arm. Gary was very gracious and said, "Yes."

I had a great plan put together to surprise her. I asked Julie if she wanted to dress up and go out to celebrate my finalizing a job. She, of course, agreed. I picked her up on the evening of April 15th. She was beautiful. We had built a wonderful relationship with the pastor at the Evangelical Free Church in Kearney where we worshiped on Sunday mornings. I told Julie that Pastor John McNeil had called and wanted us to stop by to see him before we went out. We drove up to the church and went in. His office was locked and the lights were off. I said, "Let's look in the sanctuary, it looks like the lights are on in there." We walked in the sanctuary and as we walked down the aisle, music began to play. I had Pastor John in the sound booth start the music of our favorite song, "I'll Still be Loving You" by Restless Heart.

The music was playing and I had prepared a large white candle that was lit on the altar. I had also placed three smaller candles next to it. Julie and I went to the altar. She began to cry because she knew exactly what was going on. I took the first small candle, which was yellow and lit it. I described to her how the color yellow was a color of friendship and how we had built a wonderful friendship.

The next candle was red. I lit the red candle, which is the color of love. I described how my love for her had grown and the excitement that she brought to my life. The third candle was white, the representation of the purity of Christ. The white candle had such meaning to me. Christ had died for our sins and He had to be the center of our relationship to help us through the lifelong commitment of marriage. He was going to be there for us in the good times and through the bad times. At that time, I asked Julie to marry me. With tears streaming down her cheeks and air coming out of her mouth without sound, she mouthed, "Yes." Pastor John joined us at the altar and prayed over our engagement period and our upcoming marriage.

Our spiritual mentor, Pastor John, married us on June 3, 1989, in Kearney. We truly became one. Julie cried throughout the ceremony. It was an incredible day in our lives.

Julie has been a wonderful wife and mother to our three children, Isaac, Josiah, and Hannah. Julie fills a room with her beauty. She is very soft-spoken and carries the wisdom of a woman twice her age. She is firm with me when I need to be reminded of my duties as husband and father. She is also there with a warm hug when I need a shoulder to cry on.

My emotions run from one extreme to the other—

extremely high one moment and extremely low the next. She is the stabilizing force in my life and knows me like no one else. She is the one and only woman who can meet my needs, which at times are so demanding. She is the perfect, loving, nurturing mother of our children. She gets calls on a daily basis from other mothers seeking her advice and counsel. She has wisdom beyond her years and the respect of so many. She overflows with a loving, caring spirit. Her mere presence in a room speaks louder than any words that I have ever spoken. She epitomizes the Proverbs 31 woman:

*Proverbs 31*
*A Wife of Noble Character*
*A wife of noble character who can find?*
*She is worth far more than rubies.*
*Her husband has full confidence in her*
*And lacks nothing of value.*
*She brings him good, not harm*
*All the days of her life.*
*She selects wool and flax*
*And works with eager hands.*
*She is like the merchant ships*
*Bringing her food from afar.*
*She gets up while it is still dark;*
*She provides food for her family*
*And portions for her servant girls.*
*She considers a field and buys it;*
*Out of her earnings she plants a vineyard.*
*She sets about her work vigorously*
*Her arms are strong for her tasks.*
*She sees that her trading is profitable,*
*and her lamp does not go out at night.*
*In her hand she holds the distaff*

*And grasps the spindle with her fingers.*
*She opens her arms to the poor*
*And extends her hands to the needy.*
*When it snows, she has no fear for her household;*
*For all of them are clothed in scarlet.*
*She makes coverings for her bed;*
*She is clothed in fine linen and purple.*
*Her husband is respected at the city gate,*
*Where he takes his seat among the elders of the land.*
*She makes linen garments and sells them,*
*And supplies the merchants with sashes.*
*She is clothed with strength and dignity;*
*She can laugh at the days to come.*
*She speaks with wisdom, and faithful instruction is on her*
*  tongue.*
*She watches over the affairs of her household*
*And does not eat the bread of idleness.*
*Her children arise and call her blessed;*
*Her husband also, and he praises her.*
*Many women do noble things,*
*But you surpass them all.*
*Charm is deceptive, and beauty is fleeting;*
*But a woman who fears the Lord is to be praised*
*Give her the reward she is earned,*
*And let her works bring her praise at the city gate.*

Julie is the love of my life and an inspiration to me each day. Her big blue eyes and soft touch motivate me in a way that is indescribable.

**Following are the recollections and thoughts of my wife, Julie:**

"The first time I saw Gus I was a freshman in college at Kearney State. I was walking to class and noticed a very tall, handsome man crossing the street in front of me. He was wearing a long navy blue wool coat and hat and had a backpack slung over his left shoulder. What attracted my attention was not only his good looks, but the way in which he walked. Confidence and purpose are two adjectives that come to mind. I know I remember seeing that he had only one arm, but that wasn't the reason I noticed him. At the time I remember thinking I wanted to marry a man like that someday. Little did I know...

"I was in a sorority (Gamma Phi Beta) and Gus was in fraternity (Pi Kappa Alpha) and for homecoming that year our houses were teamed together to work on a float. I was there with a friend and we were working away when we were approached by this guy, who quickly introduced himself as Gus. We noticed right away that he was a character and had everyone laughing. He didn't do any work that night, just went from group to group chatting. He was very charming and friendly and everyone seemed to like him. That was in the fall of my sophomore year in college. Gus was a junior.

"Our next meeting was about two months later at a Mister Donut shop. He was there studying and I was there celebrating a mutual birthday with a friend. We started talking and by the end of the conversation we were writing down our phone numbers for the next semester. Over the Christmas break I had the opportunity to do a little homework and asked a guy whom I had gone to high school with and was now in the same fraternity as Gus to fill me in on the basic information (was he dating anyone, where was he from, etc.). Gus had done the same for me through the same guy and thankfully after the Christmas break he had decided to call and ask me out. The date was made for later in that week for the big Kearney State vs. Hastings College basketball game. I have always been on the quiet side and was never a party girl. In fact most people who knew me, probably describe me as "religious" since I was involved with the Fellowship of

Christian Athletes and went to church. So when some of the girls in my sorority found out that I was going out with Gus they told me not to do it because of his colorful past. Well I, trusted my instincts and went anyway and am so glad I did.

"He was 'Mr. Polite' from the beginning. Opening car doors and just making sure everything was just right. After the big game we went to Taco John's and had some nachos and talked for a very long time. At the end of the night I truly knew that I was going to marry this man.

"I had spoken to my parents a few days before the date and told them I was going to a basketball game with a guy who had one arm. Later they told me they were a little nervous about this guy. Was he completely disabled? What did he look like? How would he be able to support a family? Lots of questions were running through their minds and we know what happens when we add time to those doubts, they just become more outrageous. Well, they finally had the opportunity to meet Gus a few weeks after we started dating. It only took a few seconds to erase the questions they had about his ability. They later told me that noticing how happy he made me was a key indicator in forming their opinion of him. He had quickly amazed them with his wit, charm, manners, confidence, and charisma. I have two younger brothers, Michael and Jason. They both thought he was a little quiet at first but were quickly taken with his great smile and ability to make people feel special. Gus and my brothers quickly found a common denominator in sports and since Gus didn't have any younger siblings, he enjoyed playing with them every chance he could.

"Our first date was Jan. 14, 1987. He had completely swept me off of my feet. I was so drawn to his character. He was so funny, caring, loving, gentle, patient, and motivated. He was so quick to encourage and compliment me and others around him. He was always making me laugh and laugh. It seemed like he knew everyone on campus and everyone liked him. He had an incredible faith in God and gently helped me as I was searching the Bible looking for the answers I had about God and His plan for my life. I had attended a church my whole life, but it wasn't ever much more than that—fulfilling a requirement it seemed. During high school I was introduced to the Fellowship of Christian Athletes and it was through my involvement that I began to read the Bible for myself and started asking questions about the meaning of the rituals my church had. I was also struggling with bulimia and had been since I was a freshman in high school. Bulimia is an eating disorder where I ate large quantities of food and then made myself purge (throw up). At the time I met Gus, bulimia had taken control of my life.

"So there I was falling in love very quickly with this wonderful man. My only doubts about our relationship were regarding how a talented, charming, loving, caring man like Gus could care about a girl with so much baggage. I had failed at curing myself of this eating disorder countless times through the years. I felt that I wasn't good enough to have such a wonderful man in my life. He had shown me such kindness by the way he treated me. He was always sending flowers, cards, giving me a ride to class, doing my laundry, helping me in any way he could. I knew several months into our relationship that I had to tell him about being bulimic. I remember his response was of great concern for me and wanting to do anything to help. His concern and support for me eventually did help me a great deal. A few months later I was able to reach out to an eating disorder counselor and experienced a true miracle from God as I watched the addiction that had bound me for so long finally be released. It was no coincidence. I know that as this was happening that the "lights finally came on" for me in my relationship with God. I realized that it was about the personal relationship I had with God because of what He had done for me, not the religion and fulfilling the church requirements that was important.

"By the end of my junior year in college as Gus was getting ready to graduate and move to Omaha, we knew that marriage was next. After his extremely romantic proposal, the wedding plans began. The year we had apart was horrible. Gus was working in Omaha and I was finishing my senior year at Kearney State. We shared enough good-bye tears for a lifetime.

"Gus is the most special person on earth to me. He set the tone early on in our relationship by giving me the nickname "Princess." Not only did he call me that, but he treated me like a true princess. Each day is an adventure with Gus because of his lively personality and his motivation to do the very best he can at anything in life. I feel warm in his presence because of the care and priority he has given our children and me throughout the years.

"He is always expressing his love for the children and me with lots of hugs and kisses. He is so affectionate. He is an awesome father in every way. As our first son was born I could see him trying so hard to make me comfortable and try and ease some of the pain the best he could. As little Isaac and eventually Josiah and Hannah came into the world there stood this big 6-foot-4 teddy bear with tears streaming down his face saying how beautiful the baby was and how he couldn't believe that he was a father.

"It's his character I have fallen in love with through the years. It is all about who he is when no one else is watching. His determination is played out in the way he provides for his family instead of the athlete learning how to spin the ball on his finger. It's watching him lovingly guide our kids on how to throw the baseball or shoot a basketball. I love the ideas that flow from his incredible mind. The motivation he gives me in setting goals and encouraging me in my job as a mom and wife are priceless to me. Watching him work with our children as they think through a problem or try to master something new is so awesome. I love this man more today than I thought I could ever love someone. I am so proud of what he has accomplished in his life and yet love him because of those character qualities that God has given him to accomplish so much. We have been through good times and bad and never have I had to doubt Gus's faithfulness to me or our family. I am grateful to his parents for guiding him and instilling in him the traits that make him such a great husband and father. I praise God for the gift of my husband, he truly is a treasure from heaven."

A big part of my relationship with Julie was dealing with, and overcoming, the bulimia. I remember the night she told me. I was getting ready to drop her off at the sorority house after a great date. She said, "I have something to tell you." I thought a million thoughts to myself about what it could be, because she looked so serious.

She said, "I have bulimia." I was 19 years old, and did not know what that meant. When I asked what it was she described it as a kind of disease that consisted of bingeing and purging. She had been dealing with different issues in her life and had been bulimic since her freshman year of high school. We pulled around to a side street, talked about what it was and what she had been through. It was just like the battle I had been through with alcohol, so in a way I could relate to her. That was a huge point in our relationship. All of our cards were out on the table. There were no more secrets between us. Something like that could drive couples apart, but it only strengthened our bond.

I went to the library and learned about it, and she received help through a counselor. That has since turned into a great ministry for Julie. Whenever she has the opportunity to speak when she travels with me, it is just amazing: Because no matter how big or small the crowd is, women come up to her and tell her about how they either went through, or are going through, the same thing. She has really touched and affected a lot of lives with her story.

It was just an incredible time in our relationship when she shared that with me, about being bulimic. Here we were, my scars were on the outside and hers were on the inside. Here was this beautiful woman with an attractive figure, and she was so smart. But she was suffering from something she had to get through. That really opened my eyes to something I had known nothing about. We live in a society where all the "pretty" people are portrayed in the media as being pencil thin. But one of the articles I read says that one in four college-age women suffer from an eating disorder. It tears people up and ruins lives.

When people see me, they see my scars—I am messed up physically. Yet you look at these beautiful people and sometimes lurking inside are deep problems that I pray they can deal with, and move past, getting the best of these issues before these problems get the best of them.

# 12

## Real World, Real Challenges

I graduated from high school with the intentions of a career in the medical field. I had enough experience in the physical therapy department at the hospital to write a book about it. My passionate relationship with whirlpools, leg-lifts, leg curls, pull-ups and wheelchairs seemed to be a jump-start on a career in physical therapy.

School came reasonably easy for me. Studying, on the other hand, was incredibly difficult. It was tough for me to sit in one spot long enough to relax and focus on the subject. I always felt that if I wasn't breaking a sweat, I must not have been working very hard. My trips to the library on campus were mostly futile. I went to the library with great determination and intentions. Once I arrived, I gravitated toward visiting with friends, meeting new people and shooting the breeze with classmates. I could spend four hours at the library and never open my backpack to retrieve a book. My social skills were being refined—that is how I justified this activity in my mind.

As I attended more and more classes in the detail-driven science and math departments, I realized my gifts were not in these areas. Some of my buddies were taking business classes so I thought I might give business a shot.

I thought that accounting might be fun. My first semester

of accounting was scary. My desire for accounting dwindled to zero in the first or second day of the class. Details, details, details. I knew I was in trouble on my first accounting exam when I was thirty-five cents off on a balance sheet problem and argued my point with the instructor by pulling a quarter and a dime out of my pocket, plopped it on the professor's desk and stated, "Now it balances." Needless to say, I struggled the rest of the semester.

Business students had to take two semesters of accounting to earn their degree in the Business College. This was almost enough for me to try something new. My determination and perseverance kicked in again and I signed up for Accounting II. Luckily, my professor was a basketball fan. Going into finals week, I had a borderline C/D grade. I needed the C. I learned some of my best negotiating skills at this time in my life. I convinced the professor to shoot a game of H-O-R-S-E at the gym with me. If I won, I earned a C+, if he won, he could have me all over again the following semester. This may be one of those times where someone did take it easy on me, just so he didn't have to deal with me again.

I also was taking a marketing class. Now this was fun. It was creative, exciting, and people-oriented. There were no details in marketing and there was never a black and white, right or wrong answer. The right always stemmed from, "Did anyone buy it?" My passion for marketing increased and I declared my major my junior year.

This was also about the time I was running out of money and needed cash badly. I began looking for a job that met my school schedule since I was now going to class on a regular basis. The Hilltop Mall was building an addition at the time, which was going to be a new theater. I thought this would be a great job; work during the evenings and weekends and I thought a guy could probably study during the late movie. Tim Bauer and I jumped in his Corvette, as he referred to it. It was actually a Chevette. Anyway, we drove up to the mall. The front doors were open at the theater and the light was on in a back office. We walked in and met the manager who had just been hired and was getting acclimated to the new surroundings. Tim and I asked if they were hiring and he said they were. He handed both of us applications and we sat at the counter and completed them. This was the first application I had ever filled out.

When it asked for prior employment, I wrote in my experience as one of the owners of the Gustafson Brothers Corporation.

To back up a bit, this corporation was formed by my big brothers as they built our hog operation. Dad had always been a cattleman, so it was natural that his boys loved hogs. We started with a couple of sows and held back a few from each litter to keep and breed. The hog operation grew to its peak of 16 sows. We used to farrow the hogs out in the grove behind our house. We were often up all night with them as they gave birth to their litters.

As the baby pigs were born, there were usually two or three of us with the sows. We had quite the assembly line. One of my brothers cleaned the baby pig's mouth out to ensure that it was breathing on its own, another brother cleaned the baby off with a gunny sack and my job as the youngest Gustafson brother was to get the babies to suck after they were born. The miracle of life and the responsibility of caring for others was learned on the Gustafson farm at a young age.

We loved our pigs. Each pig had a name. Our hog shed was our safe haven when we were in trouble with Mom and Dad. After I was disciplined, I made my way to the hog house with tears in my eyes. I curled up with my little pigs and told them all about my problems. I usually cried myself to sleep and the baby pigs used to curl up beside me. I was a true farm boy.

Taking care of the hogs was fun and exciting. We absolutely loved them. We also learned about income and expenses. Dad donated the corn to our hog operation in exchange for our working with his cattle. We had to buy all the protein, medications and equipment like feeders and waterers. Learning to balance the checking account, make business decisions and planning ahead were all such valuable lessons we learned at very young ages.

I will never forget the first time I went into debt. I was 13 years old and wanted to buy two A-framed hog houses to provide shelter for the sows as they gave birth. Up to this time, we were only sheltered by the nearest tree to us in the grove. Dad took me to the Farmers and Merchants Bank in Oakland where he did his banking. I had set up the appointment with the president of the bank to ask for a loan. I had the pricing of the new hog houses and a plan in which I could pay the $3,600 loan back. This was in the late 1970's and the interest rate was 18 percent. Eighteen-percent interest had absolutely no meaning to me at 13 years of age.

I walked into the bank with Dad as he took a seat in the waiting area. I went into the president's office and was literally shaking in my boots. He had a huge desk and a big leather chair with a high back. He stood up and we shook hands. I explained my need for the loan, why it was a good decision and how I was going to pay the loan back. He had the secretary type up the loan documents and I signed my first promissory note. I could barely remember how to spell my name. As I found out later, Dad went back to the bank the next day and co-signed the note.

My ego was high—I was loaded. I had $3,600. I bought the hog houses, had my first litter in the units and they worked great—perfect shelter for my hogs. I raised the first litter and the hogs grew to over two hundred pounds. The market had dropped and the prices were at a four-or five-year low of $18.25/hundred weight. I had to sell the hogs and I received my payment. I deposited the check, paid all my operating expenses that I had incurred and there wasn't enough money left over to pay even the interest on the loan. All of a sudden, 18 percent interest had a real meaning and owing someone else money was not very comfortable for me. Another of life's lessons learned.

So fast-forward a few years, back to the theater where I was job hunting.

My application that I filled out at the theater looked great! I was ready to hire myself! Tim and I handed our applications to the manager. He looked them over and asked Tim to come into his office. Tim visited with him for a few minutes and came out. I was nervous, but ready for my first interview. The manager came out and I looked him in the eye, ready to go into his office and really impress him. Instead he said, "Thanks for coming in today," and then turned around and walked back into his office.

Tim and I looked at each other and walked out of the theaters. We went to Tim's apartment and when we walked in the light was flashing on his answering machine. We both listened to the message. The manager at the theater was calling to offer Tim the job. I heard that and I was steaming mad. The manager didn't even take the time to talk with me. He saw me and thought that I was unable to do the job. My blood was boiling. I walked out and went to my apartment. I'm so glad no one was home. I had a few choice words to say about that theater manager.

After the anger wore off, I was sad. I started to think of all the times Dad said that life was never meant to be fair. The times when Dad said that I had to work twice as hard and be twice as good at whatever I was doing, just to get a shot at it. Was this what he was preparing me for? This was the first time I REALLY realized that I had one arm.

I pouted and I cried. I said mean things about the manager and I was even angry at Tim, a great friend. I was blaming everybody and anybody around me for the situation. Flashbacks from my childhood kept recurring. Each time I was down or was beaten in sports, I bounced back with a never-give-up attitude. Determined to be resilient! Determined to win in the end! Determined to be the best that I could be! Are you willing...

I was accustomed to dealing with the physical pain from playing basketball, now I was introduced to the emotional pain of truly being different in a world that likes everyone to be the same.

The next day I had fire in my eyes and a passion to find a job, a great job! The Brass Buckle was a local business success in Kearney. I decided to work for a great company and learn on the job. They had two locations in Kearney, one at the Hilltop Mall and one in the downtown area. I applied at the mall location first and had a good visit with the manager. I proceeded right downtown and applied at that store. The manager interviewed me and hired me on the spot. It was a great opportunity, a base hourly wage plus a commission on clothing sold. I was going to knock their socks off.

The people I worked with were winners. They had great attitudes. They were fun to be around, they were excited and willing to go out on a limb. I was learning firsthand why the Brass Buckle was doing so well; they had great people.

Many of the people selling on the floor had better skills

and better knowledge about clothing. I was a farm kid and the only brand name I was aware of was Levis. Matching colors and styles was never part of my life growing up. I wore whatever was left after three big brothers were done with it.

I began to build relationships with farm families in the area and they became repeat buyers. They always came into the store and asked for Gus. Selling came naturally. It was simple. Be yourself, take care of the customers and represent your employer with integrity, honesty and a top-notch work ethic. You couldn't help but succeed.

**Following are the recollections and thoughts of Jim Kolbo, manager for the Brass Buckle who hired me for my first job:**

"The first time I met Gus was in April 1986 at the Brass Buckle in Kearney, Nebraska, which I was managing at the time. I was in the basement of the store, which is where our customers shopped for denim jeans. A "teammate" came down and said there was a gentleman upstairs wanting to apply for a job. The applicant met me at the top of the stairs with a big smile and a handshake—so I knew then that this gentleman meant business. In those days I sat on a gift-wrap table in the back of the store with the applicant while we got to know each other. I have to admit that while I was interviewing Gus, I wasn't listening to what he was saying. My naïve mind was trying to figure out how this guy was going to show outfits, carry a stack of jeans, pin up displays, pin alterations, do a window display and other tasks in a retail setting.

"I had never worked with or even been around a person who had one arm. As I was foolishly trying to figure out if Gus could physically do the job, I asked a question about his high school activities. My ears perked up when he said he enjoyed basketball. I then asked him if he was good at it, Gus said, 'Well, I think I did all right; I was all-conference and honorable mention all-state.' That's when I realized I was foolish to even think that Gus couldn't do the job. We visited more and I realized Gus was one special person and his contagious enthusiasm and 'can-do' spirit was going to be a great asset to have on our selling team. I hired him on the spot. He is the only person I have hired on the spot.

"The day I hired Gus, I got a phone call from the Brass Buckle manager at the Hilltop Mall store location. He asked me what I would do if an applicant applied and several fellow employees were concerned about the applicant's ability to do the job because of a disability. I said, 'Well, if you're talking about Gus, I just hired him!'

"I hired Gus and did an experiment with Gus's training. Instead of going through all he specific product education we usually do for the first few days with new teammates, I just gave him a tour of the layout of the store, discussed the services we offer and our philosophy on how we serve our guests. The reason I tried this different approach to training was twofold. First, Gus was so driven and drawn to people coming into the store, he just wanted to start showing our products. Secondly, his enthusiasm was so contagious and I wanted to see what is greater in the equation we used in our employee handbook; KNOWLEDGE PLUS ENTHUSIASM EQUALS SALES. Gus proved to me that enthusiasm is the greater part of that equation because he came out of the gates with a full head of steam. His first three to four weeks Gus sold so well and people loved his sense of humor and his servant attitude. He then drove himself into more product knowledge training.

"Gus was an absolute riot to work with. He was always so much fun and positive to be around. He was always looking out for other people's well being. He also understood teamwork and was a tremendous team player.

"Gus and I developed a friendship throughout his employment at the Buckle for the next two and a half years. Gus always amazed me with his ability to do the job. An example of this was his ability to take a small sticky that was used to mark sizes and prices, write the information on the sticky, take it off the roll, apply it to a pair of jeans, refold the jeans and place them back on the rack. He showed product to customers with incredible excitement. He held a hanger with a shirt on it under his chin and held up a pair of slacks under the shirt with his hand.

"My favorite story about Gus and his way of living above his circumstance is the altered shirt story:

"We had a wonderful lady, Betty Mitchell, who did the alterations at our store. One day Gus bought a long sleeve shirt and he took it upstairs to Betty so she could cut off the extra sleeve so it didn't blow in the wind and get in his way. She had done this for Gus numerous times. Gus got off work and went upstairs to see if Betty was finished. He got the shirt and put it on. He walked onto the sales floor with a big ol' smile and said, 'Does anyone see anything wrong with this picture?' Poor Betty had cut off the left sleeve and left the right sleeve on! He then said enthusiastically, 'Now I will have my first short-sleeve, long-sleeve shirt!' He marched back upstairs to Betty and had her cut off the remaining sleeve and had a great looking short-sleeve shirt.

"I personally believe what makes Gus so special is his decision to have a personal relationship with Jesus Christ. Christ's love and can-do spirit shines through Gus."

Those days at the Brass Buckle are ones I will never forget. And it always goes back to when the sales bug bit me in college. I'll never forget sitting in a sales class at Kearney State. As I sat there, the instructor began to quote studies that were done on the top salespeople. He began to list qualities of top salespeople in general. The studies listed preferable hair color, eye color and physical features. Believe me, having one arm, a leg that is two inches longer than the other, different sized feet and one ear that sticks out farther than the other are not on the top 10 most desired traits for top salespeople.

I used having one arm as an advantage. Customers

remembered me. I was never afraid to call myself, "The one-armed guy." My sales approach was always built on relationships. That's what makes me tick. There were some great jokes, too.

My transition from a part-time sales person at the retail level to a full-time sales position in Omaha was smooth. The same tools I used at the Brass Buckle were also used to build businesses. Be yourself, take care of the customer and represent yourself/employer with integrity, honesty and a top-notch work ethic.

My first sales position after college was perfect. I had two markets to sell to with our product line: finance and insurance. I learned the business by asking a lot of questions of my customers. They were always more than happy to teach me all they knew. I don't remember having a plan of learning the industry like that, it was just my nature to ask a lot of questions and really understand the customer's business. Once I had the chance to get to know people in the business setting, friendships were built. Physical features never became an issue.

I gave a proposal to a customer at a bank I had been working with to sell a new technology from Kodak. Kodak has never been accused of having the lowest prices in town. I guess I didn't prepare my customer for the sticker shock very well (my fault) and his eyebrows slid up his forehead, his ears were pulled back and he gasped for air as he said, "This is going to cost me an arm and a leg!" I very calmly replied that we were having a half-price sale today and it was only going to cost him an arm, as long as it was the right arm! Needless to say, he began to breathe again and began to laugh. He bought the new technology. It was a $40,000 sale and was the second sale of the product in the United States since its introduction into the market.

**Following are the recollections and thoughts Curt Reiter, sales manager who hired me after I graduated from Kearney State College:**

"I received Gus's resume in the mail at my office. As I read through the resume the word that kept coming to my mind was "leader." He was a Homecoming King, walk-on athlete, involved with organizations, Fellowship of Christian Athletes and was working. I was ready to hire him from the resume alone.

"I called him to schedule an interview. We decided that I should drive to Kearney for the interview. I felt it was a good way to meet him on his turf. He lined up meetings with his professors and I was on the fast track of listening to all the professors' sing his praises. I did get the impression he didn't work that hard to get good grades. He had a way of 'working' the teachers.

"I felt that I had gotten the third-party references without finding out what I was getting for my money. Lots of enthusiasm, but could he sell. We rushed from place to place like two people on a mission. I like that in anyone.

"He took me to the student center where we had a Coke and talked about family. He couldn't stop talking about the impression his family made in molding him.

"We ended up the day at McDonald's on the east side of Kearney. My next test was to question his Christianity. I wanted to open the door generally if he thought there was going to be a problem working with me since I'm not the perfect Christian. This was the first time I saw his 'mad face.' Gus sat up straight and tall and looked me square in the eye and asked if it was going to be a problem for me working with him! I knew we were going to have a great relationship.

"I wanted Gus to come to my office in Omaha for the next interview. Gus quickly let me know that he had received offers from a couple large corporations. I felt threatened and didn't want to lose this guy. I worked on his desire to make a difference on the people who worked in our office. I knew he had a passion for people and I wanted to sell him on the idea of making a larger impact in a smaller company. We were a small company with approximately 25 employees.

"I was threatened by his enthusiasm. I wasn't sure I could deal with this much drive and ambition and still develop the challenge, which would keep him interested. We worked together and he was an incredible challenge for me as I was always digging in my heels and he was always full steam ahead. We balanced each other out and made a great team.

"I had been working on a business venture of my own for years. Gus decided to leave the old company and join my business venture. This scared me because we didn't have a product or a customer. Gus came to work for free and helped build the business. I hadn't built Gus into the business plan but knew he was going to push me. He was young and married and this put me in a difficult and comforting situation all at the same time. I had to decide if I wanted a partner and the answer was easy but lacked good business practice."

My first full-fledged leap of faith, without a net, in the business sector utilizing my own capital took place on Dec. 1, 1996. I started Integrity Systems, Inc. This was just another challenge that I saw in my life. I needed to go to the next level in my professional career. I enjoyed technology and thrived on the complex sales cycle. Integrity Systems set out to produce custom software solutions that assisted mid-sized to large companies to cut costs and increase productivity.

I opened the doors of ISI in December with one employee, a programmer. The business grew rapidly in the first year and I found myself running faster and faster trying to grow the business with limited capital, remaining debt-free and meeting customer needs. By late 1997, we had 12 employees and the business was just shy of $1 million in sales revenue in the first year. The momentum was incredible and there never seemed to be a lack of business, only personnel resources.

The programmers and staff were working incredibly hard. They were all self-motivated and were truly playing as a team as the business grew. The compensation program was developed to reward each person based on the profitability of the company.

Also in December of 1996, my passion to speak publicly grew and I launched Ron Gustafson—My Story in tandem with ISI. I was starting to receive a number of phone calls from schools and churches that were interested in having me speak at assemblies and youth group meetings. Each time I went to speak to the groups, I had students come up to me after the presentation and tell me about the impact that my story had made in their lives. They told me about their parents' divorce, their grandmother dying of cancer, or a brother or sister who was in an accident. They often had a tear in their eye and simply said that I gave them hope. My heart melted and I wanted to solve all of their problems, but I knew I couldn't. I could only be a source of encouragement for that day.

Both businesses were launched simultaneously and were growing like wildfire. Calls were coming in to have me speak at larger functions and meetings and I had built a relationship with a sales organization in Lincoln, Nebraska, to do the software development of the projects they sold. This became a fast track to growth by being their subcontractor. They quickly became our second-largest customer with repeat business. This allowed me to have fewer customers, requiring less of my time to manage and sell so that I could speak more often. Everything was going great, I thought.

Business was so good, I started skipping my morning workouts so I could get to the office early and get the needed work done. I was spending little or no time reading God's Word or any books. Skipping meals was a daily habit since I thought that stopping to eat would take too much time out of my day. I always seemed to be late for meetings, my kids' events and didn't take the time to spend one-on-one with my employees. It seemed as though I was in the middle of an out-of-control snowball gaining momentum as it traveled down the hill, picking up everything it ran over.

My background had always been in marketing and sales. Now my business was built on the details of technology. I missed having the fun of the sale and the chase and challenge that goes on in selling. Most of my time was spent working on the financial side of the business and putting out fires when the customers had problems. Previously when I had problems, I could work my way through them by getting my hands dirty, by getting involved directly. Since I wasn't a programmer, I could only try to ask the staff the right questions and depend on them to find the answer. This was a great growing time for me professionally, but the business was taking a toll on my attitude, patience, spiritual growth, and family life. The faster we went, the more challenges that were popping up and the less time I was reinvesting in my staff. I was running as fast and hard as I could on the treadmill of life and never making progress.

Everything came to a head May 5, 1998. I was scheduled to speak in Fresno, California, on the seventh of May, and work at the office was piling up. I went in early, approximately 4 a.m. to get the extra tasks done in the office. I spoke at a luncheon in Kearney, approximately three hours from Omaha. Julie had arranged a dinner at our house at 6:30 p.m. for some missionary friends who have been living in Spain. I worked all day, looked up at the clock and it was 6:30. It seemed like it should be one or two in the afternoon. I called Julie to let her know that I was coming right home. The drive from the office to home is about 10 minutes. I finally walked in the door at 7:30, an hour late. We visited with John and Cindy and they left around 9:30 p.m. I went back to the office and worked until midnight, came home, got a couple hours of sleep and was back in the office at 4:30 a.m. My life was being consumed by work.

I came home from the office on the afternoon of the 6th. I needed to pack and get to the airport to catch my flight to Fresno. I walked in the front door and Julie was standing at the kitchen sink doing dishes. She looked at me with a lifeless smile and the guilt just about crushed me. I knew what I was doing to her and our children. I wasn't sleeping, exercising, reading and now I was putting my work in front of my family. Julie looked at me and said, "Something has to change." She began to cry and I walked into the kitchen to hold her. I was failing in almost every area of my life, except business.

Julie and I agreed that I should go to Fresno and speak. The trip was a great success on the outside, but I was hurting on the inside. I kept seeing Julie's lifeless smile so vividly in my mind. Her pain and loneliness showed in that smile and that crushed me. Julie and I agreed that both businesses could not continue. I decided to stop speaking. I fulfilled the scheduled events that I had. Chad Pomajzl was doing the marketing in ISI and Ron Gustafson—My Story. I asked Chad not to market the speaking business any longer. This was one of the toughest steps I have ever taken to correct the direction of my life.

Integrity Systems continued on and life didn't become as simple as I planned. My heart desired my passion, speaking. I missed meeting the people. I missed the feeling of really making a difference in peoples lives. When you find your passion it cannot be smothered, it only burns brighter.

Julie and I realized what my real passion was and we began to discuss the plan in selling ISI or turning the business over to the employees who had helped in building the business. I already had been approached by two organizations who wanted to buy the business and customer base. The company we were subcontracting for in Lincoln was in the midst of a lawsuit with a distribution company that revolved around the software that we had developed. My integrity did not allow me to walk away and leave them stranded. It's amazing how you become what you say, "Integrity Systems." Two of the programmers had worked on the project and knew the system inside and out. They were also supporting the software for a 24-hour distribution company. They were being paged and even called at home in the middle of the night. Their families were being disturbed and always lived with a fear of the pager going off. This went against the grain of everything I said I stood for. This had to change and soon.

I firmly believed that we needed to find a win/win situation. Julie and I began to pray and work toward a solution. Julie and I talked about it for hours and we finally came up with a plan. I was going to call the president of the Lincoln business and ask him to hire the two programmers. This allowed him to have the systems staff in house and better support their efforts. The programmers were going to be happy because they loved to develop the systems that this company offered and ISI was in a better position to be sold.

I called to Lincoln on a Monday morning to ensure their owner was going to be in all day. I planned to make a trip to their office at noon to take him to lunch to show him the win/win plan. I also planned a meeting with my programmers that morning to discuss the projects they were working on. But they walked into my office and said they had something they wanted to talk to me about. They said they were taking positions with the company in Lincoln. I began to laugh. I felt the burden of a lifetime lifted off my back. God had performed a real life miracle, again. They just looked at me wondering why I was laughing. I shared with them the plan that Julie and I had come up with and they had beaten me to it. Here I was worrying about them and they had executed my plan flawlessly. As much as I laughed and felt the burden off my back, there was the feeling of failure once again in my life.

I went to meet with the owner and negotiate the asset values at a restaurant halfway between Omaha and Lincoln. On my way out of town, I stopped by the house to see Julie and the kids. Julie and I sat on the couch and she knew I was down. Building a business had taken so much time and energy. That business was part of me. I felt like my stomach was being ripped right out of me. It was painful and very emotional. The kids were playing around us as we talked and Julie knew I was hurting. She some how always knows exactly what's going on inside of me.

She took me into the bedroom and we sat on the edge of the bed and I began to cry. Julie put her arms around me and held me. I may be the first 6-foot-4, 220-pound baby to ever cry on his wife's shoulder. I felt weak and helpless. I always wanted to be the strong husband and here I was curled up in Julie's arms and crying. My thoughts were painful. Would this game of life ever get easy? Would I ever win at anything I tried? I was so glad that I had a wife who just held me and encouraged me. She never lost faith in her husband, even though I had hit rock bottom again.

Within a week, we had solidified the plan and many of my assets were purchased. A large Omaha company swallowed up the rest of Integrity Systems and I made sure each employee was transitioned into the new organization or placed with another firm if they desired. Julie and I were adamant about having everyone win in this situation, and they did. That was the integrity part of Integrity Systems, living life with integrity even though it wasn't easy.

My passion was alive and well again. In September 1998, I went full time on the speaking circuit and haven't looked back. My faith has grown tremendously, I work out regularly, and I feel I am doing exactly what I was intended to do; to encourage and inspire people to become all that God wants them to be. Turning setbacks into comebacks!

Being a farm boy, I was reminded that nothing grows above the tree line on the mountaintop. Farmers plant their seed in the valley for a reason. We all desire to be on the mountain top and have the mountain top experiences, but the real growth happens where the soil is fertile and can be watered in the valley. God uses tough times in our lives to build character and through character, perseverance and through perseverance hope. And our hope is in his son, Jesus Christ.

Everywhere I go, people ask, "What do you do?" I think I've answered the question a million times. I have always been uncomfortable to answer the question. Do you say you're a salesman? A developer of business-based automated solutions? A technologist? A speaker? A candlestick maker? How do you answer the question? I have finally arrived at a point in my life where I feel comfortable with the question and the answer. I'm in the people business. I have a passion for people and I simply want to assist them in becoming all they were meant to be. This is why I have written this book and why I speak to crowds all over the country. God has given me a story to tell and I simply want to share all I can about my life so that it may motivate, challenge and inspire others to overcome their challenges. We all have setbacks in our life. The key to successful living is turning the setbacks into comebacks.

People often ask me why I leave Julie and the kids and travel to speak to people across the nation. I reply by telling them about one of our family vacations.

We took the family out to Colorado one summer and rented a cabin by a lake. I woke up early one morning as I usually do, and walked down by the water with my morning cup of coffee. I crawled up on a big boulder that sat at the edge of the water. I looked over the beautiful still lake. The mountains were in the background and the sun was just rising over the mountaintops. A perfect mirrored image of the mountains were in the water. The water was like a mirror, perfectly still. Julie came out of the cabin and joined me atop that boulder and we both snuggled close together to enjoy the view God had given us to enjoy. Nothing could be said, we could only sit there speechless together. Soon, Josiah, our 4-year-old son came out of the cabin, walked down to the water's edge and picked up a pebble. He hoisted the pebble up and threw it out over the lake. The pebble traveled as if it were in slow motion over the water. It made its arch and plummeted into the water. A mighty splash shot into the air and the ripples began to travel across that big pond. What a difference that little pebble made in that huge pond. The scenic mountain image in the water was now distorted.

I simply want to be a pebble in someone's pond. If I can make an impact on just one person everywhere I go; to be a pebble in their pond. To encourage someone. To challenge someone. To make a difference in someone's life. If my life can be used to encourage someone else to take the next step. To be a catalyst in helping people turn setbacks into comebacks! What a difference that can be made in that person, in marriages, in families, in businesses. There is no end to an investment in a person. The dividends multiply through time, always with a positive return. This is my passion; a passion for people.

# 13

## You Might Wonder How or If I Can...

*Top 10 questions that people ask me about not having an arm:*

**How did you lose your arm?**

This is the most commonly asked question. Kids are very interested and honest about life. They approach me with incredible interest and candor. Usually their mom or dad is right behind them trying to put their hand over the child's mouth so I won't hear the question. Parents really have a tough time realizing that this is perfectly normal and I love to have kids ask me this question. Once in a while I will get this stroke of creativity and mention that a big bear got me or a super large dog and even Barney fell on me. I love to see the facial expressions of kids and their parents.

I always chuckle and tell them the "real story." I try to use this as an opportunity to make both the child and the parents feel comfortable in asking me the question. Without the initiative of the children coming up to me, I may never have had the opportunity to meet them. What a privilege and honor for me. I love to tell the story and I always use it to encourage youngsters to be careful around cars, equipment and other potential hazards, but not to be fearful of them. I have met thousands of people through this simple avenue.

The adults typically apologize for the children and I

assure them that it is my pleasure and that I'm excited to share "My Story" with them. Before the conversation ends I also share that the day of the accident has been one of the best days of my life! God works in mysterious ways. I know that I was the perfect boy, in the perfect place, at the perfect time. I am so glad that it was I on the fender and not one of my brothers. God picked me because he had the rest of my life charted out and knew exactly how to use me. I had the right attitude, ability and personality to persevere.

### How did you learn to play basketball?

Our entire family was athletic. If there was a spare minute while we were working on the farm, we had a ball in our hand and shot hoops, threw the football around or played catch with the baseball. If we didn't have a ball readily available, we picked up dirt clods or rocks and competed for the coveted "Most Accurate Thrower" award. We picked out a target; maybe a fence post, a tire on a tractor or a door on a shed, depending on how far away we were, and tried to hit it to see who was the most accurate. This bred incredible competitiveness in our family. This competitiveness had a natural calling to the sports field.

Before the accident, I lived, breathed and bled sports. My goal in life was to be as good as my brothers someday. After the accident, my physical body had changed, but the heart, desire and determination remained the same. I didn't realize that people thought differently of me after I lost my arm. It was still me behind the smile and my desire and determination had not been amputated or lost. Throwing a baseball and shooting the basketball were some of the first activities I did when I was released from the hospital. My dream to be as good as my brothers was still alive and ticking.

Catching, throwing and shooting were incredibly difficult.

I had to learn to do everything left-handed. There were times when I felt like giving up, but something inside of me kept pushing me to persevere. My heart seemed to say, "Just one more try." This wasn't easy, but the dream to play ball was greater than the hardship and agony of learning something new.

Julius Erving (Dr. J) was my favorite star in the NBA. He could score, pass, dribble and make incredible moves to the basket and finish with a graceful dunk. He had charisma, style and had a great reputation on and off the court. He was never boastful and always made a loud statement with his game on the court. I read all I could about him and watched as many games and replays as possible. I wanted to mimic my game after his. The thing I forgot was that I was shorter than he was, couldn't jump like him, I wasn't a pro and only had one arm and a "bum" leg. This didn't keep me from dreaming though! It's still one of my life long goals to meet Dr. J. I'm sure it will happen.

It didn't matter what kind of weather was outside. I loved to play ball. I put on my insulated overalls, my stocking cap and glove and went out onto the driveway, scooped the snow off and began to shoot. It was incredibly tough handling the ball with one hand that happened to be in a glove. Most of the time I was alone and I used to visualize myself shooting the game-winning shot in the NBA finals. I shot the same shot over and over and over until I could make it consistently.

I was very tough on myself. Excuses didn't exist and the word "CAN'T" was never in my vocabulary. My family didn't allow it in our house.

### Did other kids make fun of you?

Lyons was a small community of 1,000 people. Everyone knew me and about the accident. I believe that being raised in Lyons was another miracle in my life. The community was great and everyone rallied behind my family and me. One of the most intimidating days of my life was the day Dad carried me into the fourth-grade classroom on my first day back to school after the accident. I was scared to death at the different possibilities of reactions. Would my classmates ignore me? Would they try to baby me? Would they make fun of me? Was I different now? Who would ask me an embarrassing question?

I am so glad my classmates treated me just as if I had never been gone. They helped me when I needed help and challenged me when I needed to be challenged. What a wonderful gift my class was to me!

There have been hundreds of incidents where people who don't know me will point at me and chuckle. They will pull their arm in their sleeve and walk as if mocking me. This is a perfect situation to let go! The people who do this will never understand me or the challenges I have faced. I'm convinced that there will need to be a tragedy in their life or in the life of someone close to them before they will understand the person in front of them. And that's OK!

**Did people take it easy on you because you only had one arm?**

There have been too many times that people try to help me because they notice I have one arm. They always assume that I can't lift something such as boxes or carry my plate through a salad bar line. When I was young, this really bothered me and I was out to prove to them that I could do it. Now that I have mellowed with age, I enjoy the help and I sit back and relax and allow people to help me! People are so good to me!

My parents were determined to treat me the same after

the accident as they did before the accident. Before I went back to school, my parents met with the administration and teachers and insisted that I not receive special treatment. They were to treat me just like the other students. They were to be demanding of me, I was to finish all tasks assigned and not be "protected."

I had to learn a lot of things all over again, tying shoes and that kind of thing. I had to learn how to tie a necktie, cut a steak and eat with my left hand—I was right-handed before my accident. It was so difficult to eat soup and Jell-O—anything that was wobbly or wiggling on the spoon. I cried a lot at first and often got fed up because of the challenge. But something deep down inside of me made me face the next challenge.

I remember palming the basketball in the sixth-grade—it wasn't the size of my hand that enabled me to do that, it was the strength I had built up in my forearm. The daily rigors of farm life was a huge asset when it came to strengthening my arm to perform tasks.

I had to learn how to drive a tractor and a truck with a stick shift. It was a four-speed with an overdrive. I used my hand to shift and steered with my knee, and used my left foot for the clutch. The neat thing about my family is they expected me to figure it out. If I was out in the field and the equipment broke, I had to figure it out and get it fixed.

I had to hook up hydraulic hoses into the system in the back of the tractor. You have to pull out on a lever and then shove in on the hose to plug it in so it seals itself. I had to, with one hand, pull out and push in at the same time. I did that by pulling out with my first two fingers and held the hose with my other two fingers, thumb and palm of my hand. I'd surprise myself at times, and that sense of accomplishment only built my confidence over time.

There were a lot of times when I'd have to scoop corn. I'd grab the neck of the scoop, down by the bottom, and wedge the handle by my elbow to balance the weight. I'd pitch hay off the haystack. We got up at 5 a.m. to feed the hogs. We'd each carry our bucket of corn. The rule in our family was that we had to feed the animals before we fed ourselves. We washed down the pigs, put baby powder on them and put down new hay for their beds. Sometimes, we'd lay down and take a quick nap with them. We hated to sell them because those hogs were like part of our family.

These challenges are why I am so thankful that I was raised on the farm, because it made me stronger, physically and mentally.

My brothers were brutal. They heard "no special treatment" from Mom and Dad and enacted "he's our slave." They made sure I scooped my share of corn in the drying bin, threw my share of hay bales and they destroyed me when it came to competitive games. I can't remember beating any of my brothers in a game of one-on-one basketball. It was their intent that I had to work for anything I got.

Basketball camps were always a lot of fun for me. They usually started on Sunday afternoons and ran through Friday night. I went to the gym and always received a lot of stares. I began to shoot and often entered into a pickup game. The person guarding me sat back and did not try very hard. This infuriated me so I worked twice as hard to embarrass him by scoring on him or passing the ball between his legs. Once he became embarrassed, the competitive nature of the athlete came out and he tried to stop me. No one likes to be beaten by a one-armed farm kid! I met so many great people playing basketball. After proving myself on the court, interest was generated and friendships were built.

The pressure to perform each time I stepped on the court

made me a more competitive person and developed the determination and desire to win. This desire to win continues in business, education and many other facets of my life. When I was in sales, I entered an office or conference room and once people saw me, just like the basketball camps, they stared at me. Now, instead of embarrassing them, I made fun of myself with a joke or comment to ensure them that I was okay with being a one-armed guy. This eased the tension and we could get down to business.

## How do you...?
### ...Open a can?

We have a can opener that has a handle on it. I put the can opener on the can, squeeze the handle and then use my mouth to keep the handle tight and use my hand to turn the blade.

### ...Tie your shoe?

Growing up on the farm I used to be able to put one leg up on the thigh of the other and put the shoelace in my mouth and pull the string with my mouth and left hand. But if you've ever been on a farm you'll know that that wasn't very palatable most of the time. I learned to position the strings between the fingers of my hand to apply the needed pressure to tighten the strings. I use my thumb to hold the crossed strings while my other fingers make the loop. I then use my thumb to push the string through the hole under the loop and pull the bows. It's much easier to do it than write about it.

### ...Change a diaper?

When we brought Isaac, our first child, home from the hospital, he had his first dirty diaper. I ran into the kitchen and told Julie that "I can't change diapers, I only have one arm!" This didn't work on Julie and I had to change the diaper. It was really tough using my one hand and my teeth to hold the diaper....Just kidding! It was quite easy changing the diaper; it was the smell that was tough to overcome. I could clean out a hog house, scoop manure for hours, help a sow have her babies, pull a baby calf; but changing a diaper made me gag!

### ...Drive a car?

Driving on the farm was a necessity at a young age. If you couldn't drive you were left to walk everywhere. Dad taught us to drive by putting us on his lap and we steered the truck in the field when we were 5 or 6 years old. We progressed to steering while driving on the road and eventually he let us drive the pickup in the fields by ourselves. We were 9 or 10 at this point. My brothers and I had to drive the pickup behind a piece of equipment Dad was driving on the road at 11 or 12 years old. This gave us confidence and gave Dad a trust level that he could allow us to assume more responsibility. I drove tractors, trucks, and all the equipment before I had a driver's license.

I locked my keys in my car one day at the office. Julie was teaching school at the time and she had the only other set of keys. A gal from my office, Casey, gave me the keys to her car so I could drive to Julie's school and get the extra set of keys. I walked out of the office, across the street to the parking lot, got in her car and drove off. Five minutes later, the staff in the office said they heard a scream. They went to see what the problem was and saw Casey was sitting at her desk, very pale with a puzzled look on her face. They asked her what was wrong. She told them she gave me the keys to her car and it had a manual transmission. She wondered how I was going to shift gears and will I wreck her car. Talk about stress on the job. It didn't dawn on me that she was going to worry about that. When I walked back into the office everyone was laughing and Casey looked relieved. I gave her the keys, asked why all that smoke was coming out from under her car and why her car only went 35 miles per hour. She was pale again and I assured her I was joking!

The ultimate driving challenge today consists of driving slightly over the speed limit on the interstate in Omaha, through construction zones while eating a cheeseburger and having my cellular phone ring and having to answer it. It can be done! Did you ever wonder why car insurance is so high?

### ...Type?

The typing teacher at Lyons High, Sue Sydow, found a book on one-handed typing. She knew I was coming into her class and she had to be able to teach two-handed typing and one-handed typing. On the first day she gave me the book while she taught the other students. I half-listened to the fundamentals and read "my" textbook. My home keys are: pinky on the F, index finger on the J and the middle fingers on the G and H respectively. I use my thumb on the space bar and reach the other keys primarily with the pinky and index finger. I believe it's much easier to type with one hand than it is with two. I always thought that the second hand would get in the way!

This has been an invaluable skill to learn. I can't imagine what I would do if I couldn't type proposals, this book, letters and e-mail! I am forever grateful to Mrs. Sydow.

### ...Hammer a nail?

My brother Jim and I spent a summer shingling the roof of the huge barn on our farm. We nailed more shingles on that roof than I ever want to see in my life. I set the shingle in place and put the nail in the palm of my hand. I pushed the nail into the shingle, grabbed the hammer and pounded the nail in. I had the biggest blister in the palm of my hand that you've ever seen. Painful!

If I were nailing a board to a post, I held the board in place with my hip or leg depending on the height of the board, put the nail head against the neck of the hammer with my fingers and pushed it into the board to set it. I then hammered away!

### ...Take your kids to stores?

My three children are each two years apart. I love to take them to the grocery store to get their "free cookies" in the bakery section. I unbuckle them in the car, carry Hannah, and the boys walk right beside me. Sometimes I have to carry two of the kids with one arm—great weight training, I guess. Since we are regulars at the grocery store, people always watch with amazement at the kids because they are so well behaved. Our grocery store has a couple carts with the lower deck of the cart shaped like a race car. We alternate the race car seat and the other kids jockey for position in the top of the cart. The ladies in the bakery section always have our cookies ready when we get to the counter. The trips to the grocery store are great adventures.

### How do people react to you when they first meet you?

Introductions to new people make them somewhat uncomfortable. The most common issue is which hand to shake. Our society shakes hands with the right hand. Typically people extend their right hand. Some people leave the right hand extended so I twist my arm backward to shake with my left hand. Others fumble to put their right hand back down and extend their left hand. I am willing and able to shake either hand although I prefer to shake left hand to left hand. Dad always taught me to look people in the eye and shake their hand very firmly. This makes a statement about your integrity and character. I have been accused of having too firm of a grip! I always err on the side of too firm versus wimpy.

I had the perfect parents who were blessed to have a great capacity to teach me. I can only forward the thoughts and ideas that they implemented in my life growing up. I realize that age, background and circumstance must be considered in approaching an amputee, but the following are key in building a relationship.

■ Don't be afraid to meet him. Introduce yourself and get to know him. We can all learn from other people. Everyone is worth meeting and you are worth getting to know.

■ Don't get caught up in how to shake hands or react to the physical features! Life was never meant to be comfortable. Get out of your comfort zone and "Just Do It"! The two of you will figure it out, and you never know until you try!

■ Don't pass judgment on what he can or cannot do. You'll be amazed at what can be done with the mind and heart even though the body may appear to be lacking.

■ Don't take it easy on him. The tougher you are on him the tougher he becomes and the better off he will be. Be caring and sensitive to the situation, but don't spoon feed him life. Ask if you can assist, but don't take it for granted that he wants or needs your help. It may take longer to perform a task, but there is great pleasure in allowing him to accomplish the task alone. Sit back and take notes, you will be amazed!

Society as a whole treats amputees very well. Most people

by nature are very helpful and considerate. Since amputees are "different" than the norm (whatever normal is), they will be stared at. I firmly believe this is a curiosity issue and not mean-spirited. I catch myself staring at people in wheelchairs or on crutches because I'm amazed how they do things. This is a great way to meet people and to be an encourager. I have the same curiosity as others have.

I don't picture myself as having one arm. I always chuckle when people I know tell me they never picture me with one arm. It's a non-issue with them. They just see Gus and treat me just like they treat everyone else.

Last month, a gal that I graduated from high school with called to hire me to speak to the association she works for. She asked for a video to show the board members. She showed it at work and then took it home for her husband, who I also graduated with, to see. She called me the next day to say she never realized what I was going through as I grew up. We laughed about it because she just saw me do everything with one hand and never realized the struggles or the things Mom and Dad taught behind the scenes.

When I was a high school sophomore, a college student who lost his arm right above the elbow in a farm accident read about me in the newspaper. He called my parents to see if we could meet. He had designed a strap to assist him in lifting weights to build the side of his body that didn't have an arm. We met so he could show me the strap, but I was very uncomfortable with him. He was a wrestler and I was a basketball player. He wore slip-on shoes and I laced mine. We didn't have a lot in common and my body development was a non-issue for me at that time. We spent a few hours together and we didn't continue communications.

I learned a lot from that experience. I realized that sometimes it's more uncomfortable for people to meet "like" people. I can't push myself on other people. If they approach me, it becomes more natural.

I also realize the value of trying to develop the right side of my upper body. The muscle naturally develops on the left side but the right side of my torso (without an arm or a shoulder) has no way of developing. This creates back pain and a non-symmetrical balance issue.

I've received numerous cards and letters from people who know someone who has lost an arm, leg, is a diabetic or has other health issues. I try to correspond via mail to be sensitive to how I felt when I came in contact with my "mirrored image." My attempt is to encourage and to be available if someone wants to visit or meet. I never try to be overzealous and only meet with people when they are ready and willing themselves. This book and my video/audio cassettes are an avenue to be the encouragement in their lives as well as in the lives of people who appear to have all the body parts but may be "handicapped" on the inside.

One night as I was watching the evening news on TV, I saw a news clip run repeatedly of a pitcher for the San Francisco Giants. He threw the baseball with his left arm from the pitcher's mound and the snapping of a bone rung through the stadium. The ball ended up near the dugout on the first base line. I later heard of the cancer he had had surgically removed from his right arm and the radiation he had gone through had made his bone brittle. The bone had snapped and he had to have his pitching arm (left) amputated. A few months later I was watching TV again and saw Dave Dravecky and his wife Jan on a show. Both of them looked emotionally drained and wiped out. I could only imagine what it might be like to literally make your living with your left arm and be at the pinnacle of your career one day and have that arm removed from your body the next day!

I felt an incredible desire to meet them and to encourage Dave. I didn't know how to meet him because I was sure he was getting all kinds of requests to speak, write books and go on with life. And who was I, a farm kid from Nebraska, to think that I needed to meet and encourage a professional athlete. My desire to meet him didn't cease over the course of six months, so I set a goal to meet him. I had to get his attention somehow. Dave lives in Colorado Springs, Colorado, and I had heard through the news that he enjoyed skiing. I had an idea. I had just purchased a pair of ski gloves and I obviously didn't need the right glove. I took the right glove, put it in a box with a short note and said he probably had a greater need for the glove than I did. Julie and I organized an event that brought Dave to Omaha to speak to some of the youth in the area. I finally met Dave face-to-face. What a blessing! Dave included a chapter about me in his latest book "Portraits of Courage."

**Following are the recollections and thoughts of my friend and attorney Tom Hemphill:**
"I first met Ron on a Sunday morning in May of 1989 in a church in Omaha. The Faith Evangelical Free Church was a small church of approximately 100 people. The church was meeting in a strip mall, as it was young and growing. I had been attending Faith for about a year after moving to Omaha from Iowa. I was a single man and 30 years old.

"I was ushering in the morning service and I met a young couple I had never met before, Ron and Julie. Ron, not having a right arm and shoulder, immediately struck me. Seeing him for the first time was disarming. It looks a bit like an optical illusion since you look at him and the line that follows his neck down toward his chest and down to his hip is uninterrupted on the right side of his body.

"I see this young 20-year-old man with a big glorious smile on his face and his large frame filled up the door. He's a sight to see for the first time. I'm not sure what attracted my attention first, his big smile or the loss of his arm. He had this beautiful, trim, blonde-haired, striking woman with him. My next thought was that the girl is either his sister or this is a special man that I need to know. I know that if I were in his shoes, I would never have had the confidence to ask such a pretty girl out for the first time.

"When the service ended, I made a beeline to this young couple. Ron and I shook hands. For some reason, I did not feel uncomfortable extending my right hand to shake his left hand. I felt an instant connection with Ron. There was not the uncomfortable feeling that I had expected. Ron introduced me to his fiancé, Julie, and this gave me an overwhelming amount of information to judge him on in our first meeting.

"Ron invited me to his apartment to grill some hamburgers the next week. I showed up at his apartment and knocked on the door. I heard him say, 'Come in.' I opened the door and walked in. Ron had just gotten out of the shower and had a towel around his waist. (I still wonder how a one-armed guy gets a towel around his waist.) I saw the dreadful scarring on his lower right leg and his shoulder area. Just seeing this scar galvanized my relationship with Ron. The scarring made me step back and look. I struggled with keeping some kind of eye contact with him but my mind and eyes wanted to wander to the scarred areas of his body.

"I've often thought that Ron may have done this to me, and maybe others, to see if I could handle seeing him in this condition. I could only image the locker rooms and athletic facilities that he had been in and the amount of people that had seen him like this.

"Gus is a special person for what he has overcome. When I think of him, my thoughts go immediately to Revelation 3:14-22. John talks about overcoming. Those who overcome earn the right to sit with God on the throne. It has been gratifying for me to know that he has persevered and seeing this centered, contented young man succeed in life.

"I believe Gus and I hit it off because we were both young

farm kids working in the city and there had been hardships in both of our lives. He is a physical icon for me as I deal with tragedy, setbacks and hardships. His life exemplifies one of character, strength, contentment and triumph."

## How do you think your children will respond to their friends when they find out you have one arm?

This is a question I don't have an answer to. We will only know through time. I believe that our kids are very well adjusted and think that Daddy is very special because I have one arm. They travel with me often times to speak to schools and groups. They have heard my story hundreds of times and are very comfortable with it today. I coach their basketball and baseball teams and they think that is pretty cool. I trust that the future will be exciting and the kids will use it to teach their friends about the two major rules in our house:

1. Never give up
2. Have the courage to face the next challenge

## How do you buy shoes when you have different sized feet?

Shoe salesmen start salivating when I walk into their store. I have to buy two different pairs of shoes. My left foot is a size 14 and my right foot is a size 9 ½. We give the mismatches to local charities in Omaha. We hope that the mismatches assist in meeting the needs of leg amputees with shoes and other people with different sized shoes.

## How can you be happy having lost an arm?

I continually focus on what I have, not on what I don't have. I have an incredibly strong left arm with a big hand. I have the ability to walk, run and play ball with my kids. I have a creative mind to think through solutions. I have a desire and determination that drives me to succeed and meet each challenge. I have the greatest family on the face of the earth and a relationship with my Creator. I have so many things to be thankful for that I don't have the time or energy to think about what I have lost.

I met a gentleman by the name of John Foppe in Dallas last year. He doesn't have any arms. Wherever you go, there is always someone in worse shape than you are! I am grateful for what I have and want to use my "tools" to the best of my ability.

### Are you mad at God or anyone else?

I am quite thankful to God for allowing me to live with one arm. It has made life more challenging, I have met an incredible amount of wonderful people. I have nothing to be mad about. The places I've visited, the things I've experienced and have seen are a blessing. Who would have thought a little farm boy from northeast Nebraska would have a story to tell to thousands of people across the country.

### How can a guy with one arm hope to marry a great-looking girl?

Marrying Julie has been the biggest miracle in my life. She is beautiful on the outside and beautiful on the inside. She is the perfect wife and mother of our children. Why she was willing to go out with me on our first date and eventually marry me should be included in the largest wonders of the world.

There were a few instances where I was rejected by a girl. When I was a sophomore at Kearney State, I went to a dance that was being hosted at the student union. I was with some buddies and they went and asked some girls to dance. I was standing by myself and I knew everyone there was staring at me because I was alone. I spotted a cute girl who was standing alone as well and I got this ingenious idea. Maybe I could ask her to dance. I gracefully strolled across the floor to make my move. I approached her with great confidence and hope. We locked eyes and her eyes made their way down to my right shoulder and they lit up as she noticed I had one arm. I asked her to dance with my very soothing voice and she said "NO." I was taken back and thought that I may have misunderstood her meaning of "NO." She walked away and left me standing there so everyone in the world could laugh at me. This was another devastating blow to my ego and self esteem. These little setbacks help to solidify our character and help us to grow into adulthood.

An acrostic for **HOPE** that I learned many years ago is:

> **H**is
> **O**mnipotent
> **P**ower
> **E**ndures

Whatever happens to me, I always remember that His Omnipotent Power Endures. My hope is found in Christ and he selected the perfect spouse for me.

### Are you scared about the future and your physical condition?

Yes. I think everyone has some degree of discomfort in growing old. I'm not fearful in a negative sense. The unknowns about my leg, back and upper body are a concern. The way I deal with the concern is by exercising on a daily basis and keeping my body as fit as I can. When dealing with fear, I always take action. Action always squelches the fears and positive outcomes prevail. I have little control over many things, but I do have control over my exercise schedule and eating habits. Life is all about decisions and we need to make decisions that guide our future.

## What are you thinking when people stare at you?

I was speaking in a small town in southeast Nebraska and after I was done with my presentation I opened the forum up to questions. A little old lady in the second row chirped up and asked me how I feel when people stare at me because I only have one arm. I paused for a moment, walked over in front of her, leaned over the front row of chairs and said, "Do you mean to tell me that after all these years of having people stare at me, that it's not because I'm so handsome, but that it's because I only have one arm?" We all enjoyed a great laugh and I thought the little old lady was going to fall out of her seat.

# 14

## A Head Held High

Meeting people is a blessing that I never envisioned when the accident first happened. Recently, I was one of many speakers at a conference, and as they introduced the others, some were getting long-winded. They got to me, and I dropped my head and said, "My name is Ron Gustafson, I have a wallpaper-hanging business, and business is just outstanding. I have really been busy!" I rolled my eyes, and everyone laughed. That makes me feel so good, to make people smile and know up front that they don't have to have any trepidation about meeting me.

Humor is something that is missing in society today. We are so caught up in labels—and what is or is not politically correct—that we can't laugh at ourselves. I am not advocating ethnic or racial humor. What I am saying is that I have always been able to laugh at myself. I have made a vow to have what I call a "gut laugh" every day at work. It is simply something that is healthy—it is a medical fact that it makes you feel better to have that stress gone or reduced, and it makes everyone more productive. Each and every day is the perfect time to laugh.

When Julie and I went on our honeymoon to the Cayman Islands, there was a group of people out snorkeling. They had little bags of dog food and they were feeding sea turtles. I was feeling like a real risk-taker, so I put on my snorkel and fins, and swam out about 40 yards into the ocean where the people were. We started spreading out, and I was kind of alone. I turned around in the water... since the mask magnified everything, I was shocked when I turned and found out I was facing a sea turtle pressing up against my face. It looked huge, and it scared me to death—it must have been three feet across. I took in a big gulp of salt water because my snorkel had gone under, and I swam back to the beach—I must have been the fastest one-armed swimmer in the world! I will not let the fact that I have one arm and a damaged leg slow me down. Life is too precious to waste time worrying about what you don't have. You have to be grateful for what you do have.

I always want to be the person who encourages others. I have coached a basketball team at the YMCA here in Omaha for several years, from 6-year-olds to junior high teams. I try to focus on the kids and encourage them in what they do well, and find good in what they struggle with so they are not discouraged and know they have a foundation to build on.

I always teach fundamentals. We work on shooting lay-ups with both hands, which means trying something new for a lot of kids. This one little boy, a third-grader, went down the court during a game, and since he was coming in from the left side, he was brave enough to try a left-handed lay-up. I am adamant about the player shooting with the hand that is on the outside of the basket. This little guy went up perfectly off of his right leg and had perfect form as he shot the ball with his left hand. The ball went way over the hoop and all the way over the backboard. But I was so proud that he had done it the way we practiced, and had done 90 percent of the things right even though his shot was a little strong. I was halfway out on the court yelling encouragement to this little guy for showing the heart and courage to try this, because that showed a lot of character. So what if he didn't make it? He knew he had it in him, because he was not afraid to challenge himself.

A couple of games later, that same boy tried it again—and made the left-handed lay-up! I was more excited than he was, I think, and other kids on the team picked up on the fact that the little boy was not afraid to try to challenge himself. It was a win, win, win situation for that little boy, the team and me—as well as all the parents and the other team who was there.

Sometimes when I see other people only giving 60 percent effort it really frustrates me. I demand a lot of those around me, as I do of myself. That is something I have had to work on. I always want to stay in the encouraging mode because that is simply the best—and the only—path to success.

Wherever you go, people are watching what you do and how you treat people. That just goes back to my parents raising me in a moral and ethical climate and treating people the way we all want to be treated.

I have always been a goal setter. I remember a time when Isaac was just a baby. I was trying to workout and was having a hard time because of my knee from all the surgeries. My friend, Tom Hemphill, suggested I try biking. He brought over a bike and said, "If you like it, buy it. If not, just give it back." I took it down to a bike trail. I'd get on the trail and I'd watch to see who was in front of me. Whoever was in front of me became my goal and target. I was determined to catch him. I pedaled as hard as I could to catch him and then set the target on the next person, and then go harder and harder to catch the next person. I was getting great workouts and got back into good shape. I did not have anything fancy—just a T-shirt and shoes, no fancy equipment—but it was, like anything else, what I made it to be, nothing more, nothing less.

Being optimistic is all I know! I have a relationship with Christ that gives me hope for the future and a great inheritance in eternity. I made a decision to see the glass half-full in all situations and that I could have a direct affect on how life was to be lived.

Kids ask me what happened to my arm, I automatically look at my left arm and say, "Nothing." They then say, "Your right arm."

My focus is always on what I have, not what I don't have. It's exciting for me to get up each day and face a new challenge. It's a game for me. It is at the core of my being.

I have learned over the last few years that I'm in the people business. God has given me a gift of encouragement. My goal each day that I wake up is to be an encourager in the life of my wife, my children and the people I meet. My desire is to challenge and inspire people to become all that God wants them to be.

I have a goal to write a note each week to someone from my past. Someone who has encouraged me, educated me, or invested in me along the way. It could be as simple as a warm smile from someone and I want him to know he made an impact on me and that he is a winner in my life.

# 15

---

## A Father and Husband:
## The Spirit To Move Forward

Julie and I have three wonderful children. In 1998, Isaac was 6, Josiah, 4, and our little girl, Hannah was 2.

Isaac is an incredible little boy. He's a very good kid—almost a perfect kid. He's very obedient, and kind and gentle toward others. He's a prayer warrior, too. I remember one time when Josiah fell and hurt himself, hit the corner of the couch and had a mouthful of blood. Isaac ran to his room, dropped to his knees and prayed for Josiah. I thought about what a great lesson that was for all of us that this little boy prayed like that for his little brother. Isaac has a lot of maturity on his spiritual side. Isaac is Mr. Meticulous. He doesn't like it when other kids in his class talk out of turn or misbehave. He wants to be there to learn and stay focused. In fact, his teacher told me he has never been in trouble. That scares me a little, because I was always in trouble: My first day of kindergarten, I got in trouble for using a crayon on the chalkboard. So I believe Isaac gets his good behavior from his mother's side of the family! Julie and I were at dinner one night, talking about the kids and the future, what the kids might grow up to be. Here the kids come from the same environment, yet they are so different. Isaac is very orderly. He's so smart. He likes to think things through, see how things work. So we hypothesized that Isaac will be an engineer or an architect, someone who builds great things.

Josiah is, like Isaac, a blond-haired little boy with big blue eyes. He is a little, wiry guy who is really fun to play with. He's got a great sense of humor—he's always making us laugh. He is such a little giggle box. Isaac is like me because we eat very fast and move onto the next task. But Josiah could spend three to four hours having a good time, all by himself, eating dinner. He's just so happy. That's so neat to see—his different personality. Josiah is loving and caring. He's always got his arm around his little sister, always caring for her. He is very sensitive to people and always thinking ahead to anticipate the needs of the people around him. I have a lot to learn from Josiah. I think Josiah will be a pediatrician. He's very smart and caring and compassionate. He loves to be around other kids.

Hannah also has blond hair and blue eyes. She is absolutely marvelous. She's my little princess and is a dream to be around. She's as ornery as can be—she knows how to tug at her brothers' hearts to get them to do what she wants them to do. And of course she has her Daddy wrapped around her little finger—she can get just about anything she wants out of me. She can just melt me into a little puddle on the floor with her adorable eyes and beautiful smile. I'm afraid she will play me like a fiddle when she's in junior high. I have the hardest time disciplining my little girl. I can wrestle with my boys and discipline them, but I don't do that as well with Hannah. Julie and I always joke because Hannah is so driven and motivated that she'll be a construction site foreman, ordering the men around just as she orders her brothers around today. She's a neat little girl and the apple of her Daddy's eye.

Julie and I have special nicknames for each of the kids. These names are intended to create word pictures in their minds. We want them to be encouraged and have a warm, positive feeling each time they hear their special name. Isaac's nickname is Champ. After I call him Champ, I ask him why I call him Champ and he says, "Because I am a winner!" Josiah's special name is Sunshine. When I ask Josiah why I call him Sunshine, he says, "Because I brighten up your day, Daddy!" Hannah's special name is Princess (just like mommy's). When I ask her brothers why I call their little sister Princess, they say, "Because she's pretty like a princess and we need to treat her very special." I feel it is so important that children hear positive affirmations. We must build them up and not tear them down with negative "stinkin' thinkin.' "

Being a father is a huge challenge. My heart is with Julie and our children, yet my passion and desire to encourage people all across the country is great as well. Balancing the demands of playing dolls with my little girl to playing ball with my boys, to meeting the emotional needs of Julie is taxing. Work, community service, church functions and socializing with other married couples fills up our calendar. It is so difficult to meet all the needs and service all the demands in our culture today.

Fathering is also the most rewarding thing I have ever done, but also the most difficult. I am very driven, I like to be focused when I do something and I don't like to worry about the peripherals when I'm chasing a goal or task. Now, I am challenged because I sit down and have tea or play dolls with my little girl. Little kids, if they could spell, would spell love T-I-M-E. Kids don't look at tasks the same way we do. We just need to sit and be with them, spending time is the goal and accomplishment. I play Lego's with the boys or just do what they want to do. And that's what kids need. From my business background, I viewed something like that as wasting time. But now, I put the world aside for that precious time. It is like putting pennies in the bank for each minute you spend with the kids, and both the kids and the parents grow rich through that foundation of time spent together. That stays with them for the rest of their lives. Could there be a better investment than time?

I am also coaching Isaac and Josiah's basketball team. Isaac is a very athletic boy, very strong and ahead of a lot of the other kids—I don't say that just as a father, other people are even surprised that a 6-year-old kid is already shooting lay-ups with his left hand. I will not push him into athletics, but sports are such a great learning ground that I want to help them and encourage them.

I always want to work harder at being a father and husband than I do at my work these days. The rewards of being a father and husband are so much more important and meaningful. No, it does not come without its challenges. I come home from work and I have a lot on my mind, from work to money and other grown-up things. But how I interact with my children outweighs all that. When I'm preoccupied and my child comes to me for attention, do I snap at him because of the pressure?

I remember meeting a man who shared with me this story: If you fill up a glass to the rim and put it on a table, and as someone walks by and bumps into the table, water spills out. Whatever is in that glass spills—whether it is coffee, water or whatever. So if you have anger inside of you when you are jolted, what comes out is what is in you—anger or love. So you always want to be aware of that, because you don't want damaging words or actions coming out of you. The wrong words will leave scars on your children for a lifetime. The beauty is that positive affirming words will also last a lifetime.

We do correct our kids' actions, but we always try to do it in an encouraging way. Our rule is to give them 10 positive bits of information for every negative. Julie and I, for every "no," try to give 10 positive attributes. We have seen Isaac give that same kind of encouragement to Josiah, and even Josiah is showing signs of that with Hannah, and that's so neat to see because our kids do model us.

Isaac started kindergarten at a Christian school in Omaha. I have been blessed with the opportunity to drive him to school a couple of times a week, so we talk about what letter he's learning to write and other things they are doing in school and his friends and what he does at recess. I pray with him before he goes into the building, and we set a goal that he will encourage at least one friend that day—that a fellow student drew a nice picture or did something nice. We want him to look for those good things in other people. We also pray that he will encourage his teachers, because the teachers don't always get encouragement from young students. Julie picked up Isaac at school one day, and Isaac had told his teacher, "Thank you for being my teacher Mrs. Johnson." Julie said Mrs. Johnson had a tear in her eye. That made me proud, because we had talked about it that morning. That's exciting as a parent to be a part of the growing and maturing process. There is a lot of pain in this world, and that nice little comment or thank you can go a long way. As parents we have to be leaders and encourage positive affirmations.

As I look back on the short time I've been here on earth, it seems that the theme for my life has been turning setbacks into comebacks. The setbacks and challenges seem to overlap as they keep pouring down on me. This is exciting for me. It provides another opportunity to use my God given gifts to make something good come out of the situation.

In analyzing my past, I have diagnosed three keys to turning a setback into a comeback. My loving parents and caring brothers instilled these keys in me. They are not philosophical or theoretical. They are tools that I use each day as I get out of bed and use them continually throughout the day. Are they easy to use? No! Nothing worth having is going to be easy. Are they effective? They have been for me!

**Process the garbage**

**The first key to turning a setback into a comeback is this: Process the garbage.**

It doesn't matter who you are, what you are or where you are at in life, but a big garbage truck is going to back up right beside you. It's going to hoist up its load and it's going to dump its load of garbage right on top of you. At that very moment, you have a decision to make. You can either sit in that garbage, act like that garbage, smell like that garbage and be just like that garbage. Or you can process the garbage and turn out fertilizer and make everything around you turn green, grow and prosper.

I'm convinced that no one is immune to the garbage truck. It's going to seek each one of us out and present new challenges and setbacks. We must take on the situation presented to us and make something good come of it.

When I was running my software development firm, I typically got up at 5 a.m. and went to the gym to work out. One particular morning last year I woke up, and walked down the hallway toward the family room. I had set out my workout clothes in the living room to dress so I didn't disturb Julie or the kids. I proceeded down the hallway and across the living room floor toward the light switch. As I was walking in the dark, I felt an impact against my shin area where extensive skin grafts have been done. The skin is very thin and tears quite easily. I knew this was trouble. I made it to the light switch, turned it on and looked down toward my right leg. Blood was spraying everywhere. Julie heard the commotion and came out to see what had happened. She almost passed out at the sight of all the blood. I had walked into a toy that had not been put away. I went into the bathroom and put a wash cloth on the wound. I was rinsing some of the blood off my leg and contemplating what to do.

At first I was mad at the kids for leaving the toy out. Then I was mad at Julie for leaving the toy out. And finally, I was mad at myself for leaving the toy out. I could have placed the blame on someone else and created resentment and ill feelings toward them, or I could accept what had happened to me and deal with it in a positive fashion.

I proceeded to the gym, had a great workout and then had one of the best selling days of my career. The wound took exactly one year to heal. The healing process is tedious and frustrating, but it's better than not having a leg!

My mother-in-law is a wonderful example of processing the garbage. In 1996, Meg was diagnosed with breast cancer. She underwent a double mastectomy, chemotherapy and radiation. During the chemotherapy treatments, she had terrible reactions to the drugs. She developed blisters in her mouth that continued down her throat, making it next to impossible to eat or drink. Her lips swelled and her throat swelled to the point of not being able to breathe. We wondered if this treatment was really supposed to make her better. She persevered through this tough stage in her life and she has a clean bill of health today. She has a new lease on life. She walks two or three miles a day. Meg and her husband Gary bought a house on a lake. This had been a dream of theirs for years. She has also taken golf lessons so she can play with Gary and her sons, Michael and Jason. Through the trial, she kept moving forward, striving to see the good and overcoming the bad.

I was recently playing pickup basketball at the gym. I was

having a lot of fun and getting a great workout. I was playing defense and as I moved across the lane, my right leg was in an awkward position and as I came down on it, I felt it pop out and then pop back in. I have had enough knee injuries to know when one is bad, and this one was bad. I walked off the court and went to the doctor. They took X-rays and did an MRI. They found that I had torn my anterior cruciate ligament (ACL). The skin graft below the knee created a hazard for the doctors. They wanted to get plastic surgeons involved to assist in cutting into the skin graft so they could perform the reconstructive ACL operation. This scared me to death. I wasn't about to have anyone cut into the skin graft and spend the next year or two trying to get it to heal again.

I began to call everyone I knew in the medical profession looking for someone on the cutting edge of knee surgeries that could help me out. I ended up seeing Dr. Pat Clare, the team physician for the Nebraska Cornhuskers. He was willing and able to perform the surgery without cutting into the skin graft area. He decided to pull a third of the patellar tendon from my left knee and graft it into the right knee to reconstruct the ACL.

As the nurse was prepping me for surgery by shaving my legs, a real manly activity, Dr. Clare came in to explain to Julie and me about the upcoming procedure. He is a wonderful man and has a great bedside manner. As he was explaining the details, I interrupted to ask if this was going to leave a scar. He looked at me with a blank stare as I told him I was very self-conscious about the way I looked. There was a bit of silence, then we both began to laugh.

He cut into both knees and I was able to go home the following day. Here I am a one-armed guy with both knees being operated on in the same morning. I was a sight for sore eyes. The physical therapist came into my hospital room with two crutches in hand. I saw them and knew that this was going to be fun. I asked what the spare was for and she just looked at me. When I sat up in bed and she took a good look, she knew exactly what I was talking about. All the textbook training she had in school just got thrown out the window. I used one crutch and had a tough time walking with both knees stiff and sore.

Julie pulled up to the front of the hospital and loaded me up in the back of the van for the ride home. I sat cross ways on the floor because I could not bend my knees. We arrived in our driveway and there was the real test—the three steps that led up to the front door. I asked Julie, my 5-foot-8-inch, 125-pound muscle woman wife, to carry me in, but she didn't think that that was a great idea. I hobbled to the steps and opened my stance so my legs made a wide V. I then proceeded up the steps teetering from side to side and hanging onto the railing for dear life. I made it inside and approached the couch. Now I wanted to sit down. I then realized how difficult it is to sit down when you can't bend your knees. I stood beside the couch and leaned toward the couch and plopped down. I couldn't lift either leg up onto the couch. My boys came running across the family room to my rescue. They had those big blues beaming as each of them grabbed a leg and lifted it up onto the couch.

Sometimes we need family and friends to assist us in processing the garbage. Sometimes we can't do it alone. We need support, assistance, or a word of encouragement.

The physical therapist gave me exercises to do with both my legs. The boys asked each day if I had completed the exercises. By the end of the week, the boys refused to help me lift my legs any more. They insisted that I do it on my own. They knew when to help me and they also knew when to force me to do it on my own. That's some wisdom from a 6-

year-old and a 4-year-old!

When I was struggling to get Integrity Systems up and going I found myself coming home from work and just unloading on Julie and the kids. The stress, tension and energy involved in getting a company off the ground was incredible. I seemed to be dragging it all home and Julie became my outlet. One night as I finished "dumping" on her, I realized what I was doing. The little garbage truck was dumping on me and I was loading it up, taking it home and dumping it all on my family.

I thought about this and wondered what to do. How could I make something good out of the stress and the day-to-day failures I was having at work?

My new plan consisted of having 3x5 index cards in my car and a pen. As I drove down the interstate on my way home each night, I took an index card out of the visor and wrote down all the "garbage" that had been dumped on me that day. Right inside the house was a small garbage can. I walked into the house, wadded up the index card and threw it in the garbage can. I would greet Julie and the kids with energy, excitement and a clear mind.

Eventually, Julie and I tucked the kids into bed and I retrieved the index card from the garbage can. Julie and I sat down on the couch and I read the card to her. As we did this night after night, I realized that the perceived crisis at 5 o'clock wasn't nearly as bad at 9 o'clock. The time Julie and I spent on the couch together was truly quality time. Our relationship and love for one another grew as we shared our struggles and challenges of the day. We also realized that we were both having more and more victories in our lives than we previously thought. We must process the garbage in our lives.

Be a good-finder in every area of your life. There will

always be someone who is worse off than you. Make the best of every situation. The main ingredients in processing the garbage are attitude, attitude and attitude.

"The longer I live, the more I realize the impact of attitude on life. Attitude, to me, is more important than facts. It is more important than the past, than education, than money, than circumstances, than failures, than successes, than what other people think or say or do. It is more important than appearance, gifted ability or skill. It will make or break a company, a church, a home.

The remarkable thing is we have a choice everyday regarding the attitude we will embrace from that day. We cannot change our past, we cannot change the fact that people will act in a certain way. We cannot change the inevitable. The only thing that we can do is play on the one string that we have and this string is attitude. I am convinced that life is 10 percent what happens to me and 90 percent how I react to it. And so it is with you...WE ARE IN CHARGE OF OUR ATTITUDES.
—Charles Swindoll

**Never give up**

**The second key to turning a setback into a comeback is: Never Give Up.**

When Hannah was 9 months old, she taught me so much about that never-give-up attitude. She was just learning to walk and crawled on her hands and knees across the floor to the couch, reached up, pulled herself up and took a step. She ended up face down on the floor. She crawled back to the couch, pulled herself up, took one step, then two. She ended up face down on the floor. She crawled back to the couch, pulled herself up and took one, two, three, four steps and went head first into the wall. She always seemed to have a big bruise in the middle of her forehead. I was afraid to take her to the grocery store for fear of someone thinking child abuse.

But she never gave up. She kept crawling back to that couch pulling herself up over and over and over again. Never giving up! Today she can run faster than Julie and I can keep up with. She is a wonderful example of that never-give-up attitude. We all fail the first time we try something knew. And if you're like me, I fall down or fail, then I get up real quick and look around to see if anyone saw me fall.

As we grow and proceed through elementary school, high school and on into our careers, we somehow lose that innate ability to never give up. We learn that it's easier to give up and walk away from the challenge than it is to persevere and conquer the challenge.

Josiah, my four-year-old has that never give up attitude. Isaac, his big brother, signed up for the six-year-old soccer league. Josiah came to me and wanted to be part of the team too. Julie and I decided to put Josiah on the same team with Isaac. Josiah was the youngest boy on the team, by two years. He was slower, smaller and didn't have all the coordination that the six-year-olds had. But he went to practice each week and gave it his all. He worked very hard. It came to the fourth game of the season and Josiah was the only player on the team that had not scored a goal in a game. Early in the first half he was dribbling down the field in the open and approached the goal. He kicked the ball toward the goal and the ball went sailing past the goal and out of bounds. Josiah was so frustrated. He threw his fist down toward the ground, gritted his teeth and said "Rats."

Josiah didn't give up though. He continued to run and do his best. Late in the second half, he got another breakaway at the goal. He was dribbling toward the goal and he shot it and he scored. He was so excited. He threw his fists up in the air, his eyes lit up and his smile was, well as Zig Ziglar once said, "he could have eaten a pickle sideways." I was so proud of him. He never gave up. He was the youngest, smallest and slowest player on the team, but he gave his best at every practice and game. All of his hard work and effort paid off with that monumental goal.

I learned at a young age while chopping wood on the farm that giving up too soon is the easy way out, but also leaves a job undone. As a boy, I took the ax into the grove behind our house. I picked out a branch on a tree that I wanted to cut off. I began to swing that ax and make a minute notch in the branch. Each swing produced just a slightly larger notch in the branch. This repetition continued to the point of exhaustion. I was breathing hard, my forearm burning as I gripped the ax. My hand had a blister forming in the palm and the small notches seemed insignificant with each swing. I was discouraged as I made little progress through the branch. Just as I was ready to give up, I said, "Just one more time," and then the cracking and popping of the branch would sound and the limb crashed to the ground.

You never know how close you are to meeting the goal, to meeting the challenge. We must never give up and approach all tasks by saying "Just one more time"! Each repetition brings us closer to the successful completion to the task. "Just one more time."

## Have the courage to face the next challenge

The third key to turning a setback into a comeback is this: Have the courage to face the next challenge.

My children are the greatest teachers in the world. They

have taught me many lessons on courage and challenges. One night, Isaac, Josiah and I were wrestling in the living room. We were in a whole heap of trouble with mom, because we're not supposed to wrestle in the living room. I was attempting to stand up when I was blindsided by Josiah. I was knocked off balance and I landed right on top of Isaac. I'm a big Ka-hoona, he's a little Ka-hoona. I rolled off of him and he stood up. I could tell he was hurt and a tear began to form in the corner of his eye. His bottom lip began to quiver and he was holding back the tears. I felt terrible as I watched him run down the hallway to his bedroom. I stood up and was trying to figure out how to apologize to my little boy. What words could I use to communicate how I felt? I paced down the hallway to his bedroom, trying to choose just the right words to apologize. As I was approaching his bedroom door, he came out of his room looking at me through the big end of his Fisher-Price binoculars. As a parent, I had to correct him. I said "Isaac, you have to look through the little end of binoculars." He looked at me and said, "No, no, no Daddy, you're not near as big when I look at you this way."

What a wonderful lesson for me: How do I look at the challenges in my life? Do I look through the small end of binoculars and make the challenges bigger than they really are? Or do I look through the large end of the binoculars and look at the challenges with a positive perspective?

Our home seems to be a training ground for my children to teach me. The boys and I were in the basement last winter and they were trying to learn how to spin a basketball on their finger. Spinning a ball on my finger has been a fun trick that I have loved to do for years. They were getting frustrated and finally Isaac chirped up and said, "Daddy, you spin the basketball and it stays up on your finger forever. I spin it and it falls off over and over again." He was ready to give up.

I looked at Isaac and said "Isaac, what's the number one rule in our house?" He said, "I know Dad. Never give up." I said, "That's right Isaac. What's the second rule in our house?" Isaac replied, "Have the courage to face the next challenge." I said, "That's right again Isaac." I told him that if he kept doing his best and didn't give up, he could give me any challenge that he wanted. He and I could struggle through learning something side by side. He would learn to spin the ball and I would struggle through learning how to do whatever challenge he came up with.

Isaac's big blue eyes lit up, he walked across the basement floor, opened his toy box and pulled out his Denver Broncos football helmet. He held it by the facemask as he turned around and looked at me and said, "spin this Daddy." What in the world was I going to do now? I had a hundred reasons on why I couldn't spin a football helmet on my finger. I had a decision to make. I could tell him "No, I can't spin the helmet" or I could accept the challenge and work side by side with him. I decided to take the challenge.

Isaac gave me the challenge at 8 p.m. I tucked him into bed at 8:30 and I stayed up until 2:00 a.m. the next morning trying to master the challenge. When Isaac woke up the next morning, I showed him that I could spin the football helmet on my finger. Isaac in turn has worked relentlessly on spinning the basketball on his finger and is getting to be pretty good at it for a 6-year-old.

Challenge, as defined in Webster's New Collegiate Dictionary, is "an invitation to engage in a contest." Courage is defined as "that quality of mind, which enables one to meet danger and difficulties with firmness." We must be firm, we must be solid as we engage in the challenges of life. We must stand firm on our foundation and face the challenges with excitement, energy and a determination that can only be generated from your heart.

I believe we have to get the best out of life. This happens to be different for each person. Success isn't a person or a place; it's a journey for each of us—if we choose to walk the high road. Failure is not a person or place, and failure is not falling down. Failure is the decision not to get back up.

I wasn't blessed with a vast amount of intelligence or savvy. I wasn't blessed with a financially rich family. I was blessed with a family who gave me the tools to do and accomplish whatever I chose to do and accomplish. Each person in my family has become an invaluable building block in my life. Dad was there to save my life and carry me that quarter of a mile home after the accident. The lessons he's taught me since then will carry me so much further in life than that quarter of a mile.

Mom slept in a chair right next to my hospital bed for 42 days. Never leaving my side. Always there to feed me, comfort me, hold my hand and to rub my back. What a perfect example of a loving, caring mother.

Rick, on the other hand, was working campus security at nights while he worked his way through graduate school at Iowa State University. He had worked through the night on Friday and got off duty at 6:00 a.m. on Saturday. He drove from Ames, Iowa, to Lyons to spend the weekend at home. He slept a few hours that Saturday morning and Mom and Dad left the farm to go to the city to a movie. There we were. Rick, 10 years my senior, and myself, a very wise junior high student. I tended to think I knew it all and could rule the roost. I was giving Rick a lot of flack and annoying him in a way in which only a junior high student can. Rick is similar to Dad in that he is a man of few words. I had pushed him past the point of no return. Rick took the handcuffs off his belt that housed the security flashlight, mace and other equipment. He placed the handcuffs on my wrist and attached the other end to the refrigerator handle. Some of you readers may think that that would be a great place to be handcuffed. But when you only have one arm, you can't reach in to get anything out of the refrigerator. I was attached to the refrigerator for four hours until Mom and Dad got home. They thought it was funny, too.

Mike was Mr. Competitive. I recall playing basketball in the driveway with my brothers. I was in junior high and all my brothers were so much better than I ever dreamt of being. I could not score. They blocked my shots and I could not rebound against them. I rarely could even touch the ball. I began to walk off the court, ready to give up. Mike came from behind me and grabbed me on the left shoulder. He spun me around and grabbed me by the shirt near my chest. He proceeded to pick me up off the ground and he threw me against the garage wall and looked me straight in the eye as he said, "Don't you ever give up…..Don't you ever give up!" He then dropped me and I fell to the ground.

Jim was a senior in high school when I was an eighth grader. Some of his senior buddies had me cornered in the locker room and were teasing me and doing some mean things to me. They weren't picking on me because I had one arm. They were picking on me because that's what seniors did to eighth-graders in Lyons, I guess. They had me in tears as they were teasing me. All of sudden, my big brother Jim walked in. When his buddies saw him, they all scattered.

Dad was there to save my life. Mom took care of me and loved me. Rick was there to take me down a notch when I was cocky and disrespectful. Mike was there to challenge and encourage me and Jim was there to protect me. I have the greatest family in the world, bar none.

They blessed me with a rich inheritance of faith, strength,

integrity, character, perseverance, determination and trust. With this, I can build a legacy that will stand for years in my children. We can turn setbacks into comebacks.

I always remember what the building blocks of my life have taught me and that the cornerstone of my life must be Jesus Christ. With this foundation I can face any circumstance that may be before me and turn the setbacks into comebacks. My life verse is from Philippians 4:13: "I can do all things through Christ, who gives me strength."

# 16

## A Father's Love

My parents were very wise and they prepared me in so many ways. There were many articles in the paper and even some TV shows about me while I was in high school documenting my journey and challenges. My parents didn't let me read the articles or watch the shows until I was in college. They didn't want me to get a big head and think I was someone special or unique.

They kept me humble and focused on the task at hand. Learning to tie a shoe was one of those many new tasks. I had just been released from the hospital and had been home for only a few days. It was a Sunday morning and Mom and Dad were getting ready for church. I was sitting at the kitchen table with my leg propped up on a chair. Up to this point, my parents slid my shoe on and tied it for me. This particular morning, Mom walked through the kitchen and out to the car. Dad came out of the bedroom, handed me my shoe and said, "Put your shoe on, tie it and come out to the car. Mom and I will be waiting for you."

I watched Dad walk through the kitchen and out to the car. I looked at my shoe and wondered why they were doing this to me. Why were they being so mean to their one-armed boy? Why didn't they just tie it for me? How was I supposed to do this with one arm? Didn't they understand I only had one arm? I began to cry and feel real sorry for myself. I bent over while sitting in the chair and tears were streaming off my cheeks. I slid my shoe on and struggled to tie it. I couldn't get the string pulled tight, I couldn't get the bow made and I struggled for 20 minutes with tears falling down onto the shoe. Lord Byron once said that you can see further through tears than a telescope. Twenty minutes later the shoe was tied, I got in the car and we were 20 minutes late for church that morning. It was a long, silent drive to church. I know as a father today that it was 100 times more difficult for my parents waiting for me in the car than it was for me tying my shoe.

My life is scattered with these stories where my family prepared me for the "real world."

As you might have gathered, my father's impact on my life has been tremendous.

Dad is somewhat intimidating to most people. He stands 6-feet, 6-inches tall and weighs about 265 pounds. He wears a size 15 shoe and his hands are monstrous. His complexion is rough from all of the years sitting out on open tractors in the field. His skin is like leather, dark and worn. He seems to carry a very serious look on his face most of the time. My coaches and friends were somewhat fearful of this gentle giant. He is a man of few words so most people didn't really know him.

His serious and intimidating exterior never fooled his family. He loved to laugh, often times until tears came to his eyes, and loved to be rough as we wrestled. My brothers and I had an incredible amount of respect for Dad. He was a disciplinarian. He believed that obedient, well-behaved kids would have a bright future.

Whenever we got into trouble as young kids, we always wanted Mom to spank us. It was a family joke that we all pretended to cry after she spanked us, then we ran to our room and laughed. "We got away with that one!" we said. Mom eventually caught on to this and said, "Wait until your father gets home!" This put the fear of God in us. We would go into the bathroom and get wash cloths or whatever we could think of and put them in the seat of our pants, hoping this would insulate the sting we were anticipating. Dad would arrive home and Mom would call for us. We shed tears of regret as we walked up to Dad. We knew we were going to suffer the consequences of our actions! We would have to explain the trouble we were in to Dad and his eyes would literally burn a hole right through us. We melted to a grease spot on the floor. His hand was so big. When we received our due punishment, usually just one spank, his hand would literally cover our bottoms and wrap around us and his fingers seemed to touch in the front. We cried for hours. Our feelings hurt more than our bottoms. Dad always came into our rooms, visited with us and would end each discussion with a hug. I always knew the hug was coming, but the disappointment I felt waiting for it was a learning experience. I never lost that respect for Dad and never will. He's a loving, caring, teddy bear with high standards, character and insights.

My brothers and I used to get a lot of laughs from Dad. We would be out in the field and Dad was in the tractor with a cab on it. He often wanted us to move a wagon or a truck to another location and he began to give us these hand signals from inside the tractor. How a man that could articulate a message so well verbally could give such a garbled mess in hand signals we'll never know. My brothers and I saw his signals then looked at each other and shrugged our shoulders, not having a clue what he was trying to communicate. We looked back at Dad and saw his face getting red and the veins popping out of his forehead in anger. Once we knew he was mad, we guessed at what he wanted. As we got older, this became a great game to aggravate Dad with. We continued to act like we didn't know what he was signaling and not move. My brothers and I then verbalize to each other, in a mocking tone, what he was saying. His fist in the air moving in a circular manner meant, "I'm going to tie spaghetti around your neck and choke you when we get home." His finger pointed to the south in August meant, "It's really cold in this air-conditioned cab and I don't want to open the door and let the hot southerly winds blow in here." We used to bust a gut laughing and Dad got so frustrated with us. No wonder his blood pressure was always so high.

Having been an athlete himself, he was like having a coach around all the time. He made a basketball hoop for us on the side of the driveway that could be lower or raised to varying heights. This was over 20 years ago before the "modern" hoops were made. Dad cut the backboard out of plywood, attached the rim and bolted a piece of plate iron to the back of the plywood. He made a ninety-degree angle in the pipe that ran down into a larger piece of pipe that was set into cement in the ground. Two bolts in the large pipe would be tightened or loosened to move the basket up and down.

Dad always had great ideas for me to try. He demonstrated them for me and then had me try it. He never pushed me past the point of being discouraged. He always left the decision to pursue the task at my own speed.

As I grew and began to play organized baseball with a cast on my leg, he came up with another great idea. I had always been a pitcher or catcher. Since my right leg sported a cast from my toes to my hip, I was smart enough to realize that the catcher position might not be a great idea. But pitching was going to be perfect. I began to work on my control and speed pitching with my left arm. Dad had to continue to get his farm work done and couldn't meet my insatiable desire to play hour after hour. This is when he built the pitching backstop with the mattress. When he was finished constructing the backstop, he looked at me, smiled and said, "throw till your heart's content"!

I spent hour after hour throwing at that mattress, often times not hitting it, but the shed behind it. My control kept getting better with each trip to the mattress with my bucket to pick up all 12 balls.

Dad was a master motivator as well. My brother Jim was a great leaper. He had a 39-inch vertical jump and could literally jump out of the gym. He high jumped seven feet in college. He was five years older than I was and I spent a lot of time in his big footsteps. I wanted to jump like he did. My God-given tools weren't quite as polished as his were though. My vertical jump with my 35-pound plaster cast on was about three inches, but my desire was great. I hobbled through a doorway and tried to touch the top of the door frame. I jumped hundreds of times off my left leg and reached with my left hand, which is awkward at best. But with the condition of my right leg, this was going to be the best I was ever going to be able to do, so I might as well get used to it.

But as I grew, my goal changed from the door frame to the ceiling. I was getting close, but couldn't quite get there. Dad must have sensed that I was getting frustrated. He took a pack of cigarettes out of the cabinet, got a roll of Nebraska chrome (duct tape) and taped the package on end to the ceiling. This became my intermediate goal. I hobbled across the living room floor by hopping on my left leg twice, planting my right leg, then hopping on my left leg twice again, jumping off my left leg and would just miss the cigarette package. Then I'd try it all over again, hour after hour. People came to our house and looked very curiously at that pack of cigarettes hanging from the ceiling. Dad said it was just one of Ronnie's goals.

This was the method Dad used to educate me about setting high goals, achieving high goals and setting more goals. Talk about crystallizing the concept of goals for a young boy.

Dad's presence in my life was indescribable. He was intense when it came to his boys performing at a high level on the athletic field. As a youngster, I remember my brothers coming home after their basketball games and Dad reviewing the game with them. It made him sick to see one of us miss an easy lay-up shot. He was a stickler on fundamentals. He said, "If you can't make a lay-up, you shouldn't be playing." Dad got his blood pressure up after games and we all sat around the kitchen table and listened to his rendition of the game. He used the salt and pepper shakers, ketchup bottles and glasses to demonstrate pick and rolls and other maneuvers on the court as he saw them. It was fun for me to see that big vein in his forehead grow larger and larger the longer he talked about the game. We often wondered if we were at the same game Dad was on some nights.

By the time I got to high school, I knew what to expect after the games. During my games, it was amazing how I knew exactly what Dad was thinking as he sat in the stands. He rarely talked to anyone there because he was watching and studying the game intently. The crowd could be yelling and the music blaring, but somehow, I could hear Dad clear his throat with a cough as if he were right next to me. He had a distinctive, smoker's cough and I could hear it loud and clear wherever I was. I could tell if he were pleased or not by the tone of his cough. When there was a time out, I ran to the huddle and took a quick glance at Dad. We locked eyes and I instinctively knew what I needed to do. I think Dad and I communicated at a deeper level than most fathers and sons, and most of the communication was non-verbal.

Dad carried me everywhere when I got out of the hospital

because I had a splint on my leg and couldn't walk. He placed his left arm under my two legs and his right arm around my waist. I put my left arm up around his neck and held him. He hoisted me up and carried me to the kitchen table for meals, to the car for errands or trips and from the car into school. As a 9-year-old little boy, I was often embarrassed by being carried around by my Dad. But yet those were such fond, warm, loving memories. Today, who wouldn't give their right arm to have such great memories of their Daddy! So many people don't have the ability to understand the love that the Father in heaven has for them because of how they view their earthly father. The earthly example my father gave me could not be any clearer of my Father in heaven. When I daydream and think about Dad today, this is how I see him, with his arms lifting me up and my arm wrapped around his neck holding him close, relying totally on his strength to carry me.

I cannot imagine what my father has been through. The thoughts that must have run through his mind as he carried me that quarter of a mile back to the house after the tractor left its mark on me for life. As a dad today, it's incredibly difficult to see my little 2-year-old daughter fall off the swing, or my 4-year-old son fall on his bike, or 6-year-old get hit in the head with a baseball. The heart-wrenching pain that I have when I see my kids cry is incredible. But this is nothing compared to what my Dad went through. The feelings of guilt, the "Why Ronnie and not me?" and, "I killed him."

Dad experienced nightmares for more than 20 years. He'd wake in the night screaming and sweating, reliving the accident in his mind over and over. His emotional pain was so much greater than my physical pain. Nothing can compare to the pain he went through. Even today as we visit about the accident, his eyes well up with the tears and he will leave the room to clear his head. This pain is deep-seated. Never easy to relive. Impossible to forget.

Dad was very wise. He taught me how to think. He taught me how to plan ahead. He taught me how to respect and honor life. He taught me to care for our animals on the farm before myself. He taught me how to make eye contact with people, how to shake hands, how little boys are to be seen and not heard when adults are talking. He taught me to believe in myself. He taught me that all things are possible if I was willing to pay the price. He loved me unconditionally. He disciplined me when I needed discipline. He encouraged me when I needed encouragement. He prepared me for the "real world" where not all things are fair and just. As I write this, my eyes are filled with tears as I crystallize the impact that Dad made on my life. Words can never express his lasting impact on me.

My desire is to be just half the father to my kids as Dad was to me. Dad is and always will be my hero. Simple and clear, he's the best dad in the world. Thank you, Dad.

As parents, friends, neighbors, relatives or spouses, we must realize that dreams are born from the soul, and live day to day in our hearts. My parents, my brothers, friends, my wife and our children all have dreams, as do I.

You and your loved ones have dreams. Be an encourager. Be a building block in someone else's dreams. When you assist people in reaching their goals and dreams, they will in turn, assist you in obtaining your goals and dreams.

We all get down at various points in our life, but we must overcome the obstacle in front of us. It may be cancer. It may be the loss of a limb. It may be a loss of a child or parent. Whatever your setback is today, turn it into a comeback. No one is up 100 percent of the time. I know I get down at times. There is a song I listen to before every presentation I give that keeps my mind clear and focused. The words by Twila Paris are as follows:

**The Warrior is a Child**

Lately I've been winning battles left and right
But even winners can get wounded in the fight
People say that I'm amazing
Strong beyond my years
But they don't see inside of me
I'm hiding all the tears

They don't know
That I go running home when I fall down
They don't know
Who picks me up when no one is around
I drop my sword and cry for just awhile
'Cause deep inside this armor
The warrior is a child

Unafraid because His armor is the best
But even soldiers need a quiet place to rest
People say that I'm amazing
Never face retreat
But they don't see the enemies
That lay me at His feet

They don't know
That I go running home when I fall down
They don't know
Who picks me up when no one is around
I drop my sword and look up for a smile
'Cause deep inside this armor
Deep inside this armor
Deep inside this armor
The warrior is a child

The garbage truck is going to find you and eventually dump on you. Your desire, determination and passion to reach your goals must be intense. If you are down, if you have been dumped on and you're on the verge of throwing in the towel, never give up! You can do it! You have all the tools that are needed to face life head on. You are fully armed! Just give it one more try. If you don't have someone there to cheer you on at this very moment, look at the cover of this book, look deep into my eyes and listen very carefully as I say to you, "I believe in you. You can do it. Never give up!"

Can you? Yes you can. You are a winner! You are fully armed for success!

### Romans 5:3-5 (NIV)

*"Not only so, but we also rejoice in our sufferings, because we know that suffering produces perseverance; perseverance, character; character, hope. And hope does not disappoint us, because God has poured out his love into our hearts by the Holy Spirit, whom he has given us."*

If you would like to have Gus share his story of turning setbacks into comebacks at your annual meeting, awards banquet, sales meeting, church or school, please call:

(Toll Free)
1-877-780-4068
or
E-mail
gus_ gustafson@msn.com

Name:_____

Company:_____ Title:_____

Address:_____

_____ Phone:_____

City:_____ State:_____ Zip Code:_____

Is the above address your: ☐ Business Address? or ☐ Home Address?

| ITEM | TITLE | QTY | PRICE | TOTALS |
|------|-------|-----|-------|--------|
| Book | *Fully Armed* | | **$12.95** | |
| Video Cassette | *Turning A Set-Back Into A Come-Back* | | **$29.95** | |
| Audio Cassette | *Turning A Set-Back Into A Come-Back* | | **$14.95** | |

**\*Shipping/Handling**
Single item order:           **$3.50**
Order 2 - 5 items:          **$5.00**
6 items or more = **$5.00** *per multiples of 5 items or any fraction thereof*

**SUBTOTAL:** $

NE residents add 6.5% sales tax: $

\*Add shipping / handling: $

**TOTAL:** $

For more information on resources,
please call: **1.877.780.4068**

Mail today (<u>checks</u> and <u>money orders</u> payable to)
**RON GUSTAFSON – MY STORY**
3313 South 89th Street • Omaha, NE 68124

*Please allow 2-3 weeks for delivery.*

---

Name:_____

Company:_____ Title:_____

Address:_____

_____ Phone:_____

City:_____ State:_____ Zip Code:_____

Is the above address your: ☐ Business Address? or ☐ Home Address?

| ITEM | TITLE | QTY | PRICE | TOTALS |
|------|-------|-----|-------|--------|
| Book | *Fully Armed* | | **$12.95** | |
| Video Cassette | *Turning A Set-Back Into A Come-Back* | | **$29.95** | |
| Audio Cassette | *Turning A Set-Back Into A Come-Back* | | **$14.95** | |

**\*Shipping/Handling**
Single item order:           **$3.50**
Order 2 - 5 items:          **$5.00**
6 items or more = **$5.00** *per multiples of 5 items or any fraction thereof*

**SUBTOTAL:** $

NE residents add 6.5% sales tax: $

\*Add shipping / handling: $

**TOTAL:** $

For more information on resources,
please call: **1.877.780.4068**

Mail today (<u>checks</u> and <u>money orders</u> payable to)
**RON GUSTAFSON – MY STORY**
3313 South 89th Street • Omaha, NE 68124

*Please allow 2-3 weeks for delivery.*